PARISWALKS

PARISWALKS

CLOSE-UPS OF THE LEFT BANK

Alison and Sonia Landes

THE NEW REPUBLIC BOOK COMPANY, INC.
Washington, D.C.

Published in the United States of America in 1975
by the New Republic Book Company, Inc.
1826 Jefferson Place, N.W., Washington, D.C. 20036

Library of Congress Cataloging in Publication Data

Landes, Alison, 1953-
    Pariswalks: close-ups of the Left Bank.
    Includes index.
      1. Paris—Description. I. Landes, Sonia,
1925-   joint author. II. Title.
DC707.L28 1975   914.4'36   75-8699
ISBN 0-915220-02-4

Printed in the United States of America

Jacket design by Peter Provenzale
Text design by Hugh Leckie
Cover photo of authors by Paul Koby

Photographs by Anne Peretz

To David, *Père de famille*

Preface

In this book we offer you step-by-step tours of four of the oldest and most fascinating neighborhoods of Paris: La Huchette, St. Julien le Pauvre, St. Germain des Prés, and Mouffetard. The two-and-a-half-hour walks, which cover an area of approximately five blocks each, will make you a connoisseur of these neighborhoods. What is hidden to the casual observer becomes the key to Paris. Through the signs and stories of the past, the architectural details, and the life of today, the city unveils itself. The acquisition of this knowledge makes you a friend and possessor of the *quartier* forever.

We feel that this represents a significantly different approach to travel. The typical visitor to Paris, relying on conventional guidebooks, does his best to make the most of his time by taking in the tourist "musts." He may not be able to match Art Buchwald's "5-minute Louvre," but he gives it a quick going-over between the Arch of Triumph and the Eiffel Tower. He does "Paris by Night" and takes the bus tour to Versailles. All of these things are, as the Michelin guide puts it, worth the trip, but neither separately nor together do they constitute a visit to Paris.

Most guidebooks cater to this restless quest for historical and artistic monuments. The museums they detail with such care are full of beautiful things lifted out of context and presented in necessarily artificial settings. There is nothing French about the Venus de Milo or Mona Lisa; indeed, the

latter was part of the enormous loot carried home from Italy by
French invaders in the 1790s, and to this day the Italians would
be very happy to have it back. The great cathedrals that are
among the jewels of Europe's architectural and spiritual
heritage have long survived the society that built them and
stand out from the houses and streets around them like isolated
monuments of the past. They could as easily be out on the
Burgundian plain, like the basilica at Vézelay, as on the traffic-
ridden Ile de la Cité in the heart of Paris.

Even those guides that try to assist the visitor to know a place
by walking the ground take him from one point to another so
quickly that he can obtain at best a passerby's impressions.
Here, for example, is the way one otherwise excellent book
covers one of the most fascinating, animated streets of the
medieval Latin Quarter: "From the modern Place St. Michel let
us follow the Rue de la Huchette, pausing on the way to look
along the picturesque Rue Zacharie and the Rue du Chat qui
Pêche, which got its name from an old shop sign." One sentence
for one of our walks; an area that has as much or more to tell
about Paris than any of the formal monuments and handsome
perspectives that are the usual tourist fare.

There is another strategy to visiting a city—what we call
close-up tourism. We want to make you feel, if even for a short
time, a part of Paris—someone who gets to know a piece of the
city intimately, shop by shop, house by house. We have chosen
for the purpose quarters where many of the streets are still
the narrow, irregular, meandering paths of medieval and early
modern times. These four quarters on the Left Bank of the
Seine have by the accidents of history been preserved, though
continually threatened, from the hammer and shovel of urban
planner and builder of boulevards.

The fact that these neighborhoods have been spared the
demolition and monument-building that has transformed most
of old Paris has not stopped them from changing over time, but
at a different rhythm. They are not fossils, but living, active
microcosms of Paris. The visitor who looks at them with a
careful, unhurried, curious eye can peel off layer after layer of
the past and read them like a live archaeological dig. By
comparison, much of Paris is shallow—a construct of the
nineteenth and twentieth centuries. These other, newer
neighborhoods have their own interest, but there is a
homogeneity and imitation about them that excludes the

spontaneity and ability to surprise of the older city.

No matter how often we researched our walks, we never failed to make a new discovery. We served as constant guides for an entire year to visitors from all countries, student groups from junior high school to college, and French friends, all of whom shared our excitement and to our surprise and delight found things we had not yet noticed. One friend said she would never walk down a street in the same way again. We expect this to happen to you, and we would be pleased to hear about your discoveries.

On these walks you may sit, stand, snack, lunch, or dine. Eating places have been carefully chosen for their interest as well as their cuisine. We had the rare experience of watching the chefs at work and offer you some excellent recipes, which we feel are the best reminders of your visit to Paris. We have made only those changes necessary to succeed in the United States. The walks are free. They are arranged for the comfort of nonwalkers—like us—as well as walkers. Most of the people in these areas know us well and will be happy to speak with you, and our maps and pictures should guide you without difficulty. At the end of this book we have included a glossary of French words, a chronology of important historical events, and lists of hotels and restaurants. It is wise to read each walk before setting out in order to plan your day more effectively.

Go walking in Paris—the city will never be the same again.

A few words about how we came to do this book:

One summer before leaving to spend the year in Paris we decided that since we were already a sort of agency for advice about the city, we ought to put it in writing. We felt eminently qualified: We had lived in Paris on and off for a total of five years, the children went to school there, one of them was even born there. We had first gone as a family in 1948 because David, the père de famille, had to finish his PhD in French history. That was when Pierrette Coadou, a wonderful Breton lady, came to live with us, and she has helped keep the French feeling alive in the household ever since. That was the beginning; since then David's research and teaching have taken us back innumerable times.

I (Alison) was graduated from Sarah Lawrence in May 1975 and, despite a heavy concentration in Proust and Balzac, am currently pursuing a career as a jeweler/silversmith.

I (Sonia), after having taught reading in the first grade and literature in the twelfth, am now writing about children's literature and training teachers in this field.

Everyone was surprised that a mother and daughter were able to work together easily and successfully. We were asked questions like, "Do you still talk to each other?" "Who did the writing?" "Who did the research?" and so on. "Yes, we still talk," all the time, and we both shared all the work. Although our styles differ—one is more friendly and will talk to anyone, one is a stickler for accuracy in every statement—we are still able to combine our efforts by dint of tugging, hauling, and lots of laughing.

Acknowledgments

We would like to thank all our friends who came to visit, and who were willingly or unwillingly dragged out into the streets of Paris to test our walks with us, and all those who read the manuscript, for their encouragement and helpful advice: Richard Landes, Mickey and Phyllis Keller, Janis Bookman, Deborah Kahn, Marie-Madeleine Berry, Arthur and Ina Rifkin, Cyrille and Jack Fuchs, Edward and Jane (née Landes) Foster, Michael and Jacqui Goldmann, Leonard and Marcia Zigelbaum, Judith and Morton Berkun, Henry and Nitza Rosovsky, Fritz and Peggy Stern, Françoise Crouzet, Debra Seltzer, Fred Landes, Kathy Harris, Sandy Harrison, Cathy Dean, Laurie Dietz, Liz Wolsky, Josie Vernon, Julie Rodwin, Patricia Scanlon, Jane Appleton, and a special thanks to Pierrette Coadou who helped us with the cooking and anything else that came up. Most important of all, we thank David who read every word we wrote with a discerning eye, and always told us we'd be a big success.

Contents

PARISWALKS

ADVICE, TIPS, INFORMATION, AND PERSONAL BIASES

Read this section carefully before starting your trip.

HOTELS

We are pleased to report that hotels in France represent one of the better buys in Europe. The deluxe hotels are stunning, the first class ones, superb, and the moderately priced hotels are not only very comfortable, they have such a distinctive style you will find yourself planning to return to the same one over and over again. Whatever hotel you choose, ask for a room on the courtyard. Paris is a busy city and wakes up early, so you want to get away from the noise. Taxes are always included in the price of the room: service 15 percent most of the time, and breakfast some of the time. Check on these arrangements beforehand. Breakfast is continental, which means *café au lait*, tea or chocolate, and croissants (if you're lucky) or a roll and butter and jam. The French don't eat American- or English-style breakfasts, and only hotels with kitchens could oblige you. It is wise, anyway, to adjust your eating habits to the country you are visiting.

The old horror stories about antiquated French plumbing are no longer true. On the contrary, when the French do a modern bathroom they go to excess and cover the walls from top to bottom with inch-square pastel-colored tile. The ever-present *bidet* serves not only its intended purpose, that of washing private parts, but also for rinsing out a few things, keeping bottles warm or cold, or soaking tired feet.

Make the most of your hotel by getting the staff to help you in all kinds of ways. The man at the desk is the one to speak to. He'll take messages, give you directions, hold your luggage, mail your letters, and help you make telephone calls. The larger hotels have a concierge with a desk of his own. In addition to the regular services he will arrange for theater tickets, transportation, and might even wrap a package and mail it home. If the concierge has helped you in some special way, he rates a special tip when you leave.

TRANSPORTATION

There are five ways to get around Paris; each has its advantages and drawbacks. The first and best method is, of course, your own two feet. People-watching, window-shopping—in short, real contact with the city—is only for pedestrians. Feet, however, tire and blister, so wear the most comfortable shoes you already own. Watch where you put your feet. The scattering of dog droppings is so ubiquitous that we were forced to walk with one eye on the pavement at all times. Paris traffic is another problem for the pedestrian. If you are at all timid, stick to the crosswalks and cross with the light.

Taxicabs are another method of transportation; the rates vary with the time and place. In Paris, from 6:30 a.m. to 10:30 p.m., the driver should use tariff A, from 10:30 p.m. to 6:30 a.m., tariff B.* Not every driver is honest, and tourists are easy victims. The most common trick is the long, unnecessary detour, which can be guarded against by following the route with a map so that you have some idea where you're going. It is also a good idea to mention the denomination of any large bill used in payment at the time you hand it over. (It's a good idea in shops as well.) We stress the hazards, but there are compensations. Some French cabs are simply a pleasure to ride in, so that getting there is half the fun. Before you leave Paris, you must hail a Citroën DS. The miraculously suspended seats feel like floating sofas.

Private (or rented) cars are also a possibility, but unless you know Paris well, we would not suggest using them. In addition

---

*In the suburbs, even if part of the ride is in Paris, the driver should use tariff B from 6:30 a.m. to 10:30 p.m. and tariff C from 10:30 p.m. to 6:30 a.m. The tariff will also change coming or going to the airport; the boundary is the Blvd. Périphérique.

to getting around one-way streets, there is the special hazard of the French system of priority for the car on the right. This is much more strenuously cherished than similar practices in the United States, and it reaches absurd proportions in large traffic circles like the Etoile (where the Arch of Triumph is located). Rumor has it that some inexperienced drivers have been trapped there for hours, unable to get across the streams of incoming cars.

Parking is almost impossible in Paris, and the French will leave their cars anywhere, blocking your car or even your doorstep, but the police occasionally retaliate by fastening a *sabot,* or "shoe," on to the wheel of illegally parked cars. This is a huge clamp that prevents movement and must be removed by the police, who collect a fine on the spot. If this happens to you, just pay up. Avoid getting involved in anything official with the police or the government.

The best way to cover long distances in Paris is to take either buses or the métro. The advantage of the bus is that you can see where you are going. You are, however, caught in the same traffic that a taxi is. There are bus maps available, but in any case your hotel concierge or a policeman will be able to help you. Bus stops are signaled by a round red-and-yellow sign affixed about 10 feet above ground and listing the numbers of all buses stopping at that point. Be sure to flag down the numbered bus you want, however, or it won't stop for you. On each bus pole there is also a plate (about five feet above ground) listing the names of every stop along the route. This listing is divided into *sections,* and if your ride is longer than one full *section,* your fare will be two tickets (the maximum) instead of one. The plate shows by a red line the distance you can travel for one ticket. You use second-class métro tickets or buy tickets on the bus, although they cost more in the second case. You are required to punch your ticket yourself, in a machine placed near the door for that purpose. Do this, and then hang on to your ticket(s), because there are occasional *contrôles,* when officials come by to check their validity. Some buses stop running around 9:30 p.m.; night and Sunday service is irregular. The plate at the bus stop will tell you this as well.

The Paris métro is a marvelous invention and well worth using. It covers almost every square inch of Paris with all deliberate speed and efficiency. Buy a booklet, or *carnet,* of 10 tickets; second class, 8 francs; first class, 12 francs. (The differences between first and second class are the upholstery on the seats and the size of the crowd at rush hour.) Finding your way is not at all difficult. The métro walls are covered with maps, some that even light up your route electrically when you press the button for your destination. Find where you are and the stop that you wish to get to; then trace the route, picking out the terminal stops, which will be the name of your *direction* on each line. For example, if you are at Opéra and want to get to St. Germain des Prés, you would go four stops to Châtelet in the *direction* Mairie d'Ivry. There you would change, following the signs that read *correspondance* (*sortie* means "exit") till you found the signs for *direction* Porte d'Orléans. On this line you would go four stops to St. Germain des Prés. Everything is clearly marked, and even though in some stations you may feel you've covered a mile of hallways and staircases, do not despair. Hurry along with the French, and you will arrive, no doubt just in time for the automatic doors to close in front of you, keeping you from entering the *quai* just as the train tantalizingly draws into the station. When you are finally on the *quai* and the train pulls into the station, lift the latch of the compartment and slide them open—these doors are not automatic—or get behind someone who will do the job for you. When you want to get out of the train, having arrived at your stop, do the same. On a few lines, there are new-model (very quiet) cars, where it suffices simply to lift the latch to open the doors. The métros run until 12:30 or one in the morning, depending on the line, and are safe to use anywhere, anytime.

Paris as a whole is extremely safe; a policeman or two on every corner in certain *quartiers* eliminates fear and danger. Alison has been known to walk alone in the small hours unharmed and unafraid. **A note to women who are followed and bothered:** You are only being teased, and you are not in any danger. If you turn around, however, and slap a man, he'll surely hit you right back. The best technique is to behave as coldly and silently as possible—the men are usually easily deterred and are not after you, but after anything female.

If you are staying in Paris a week or longer we would recommend investing in the invaluable *Paris par Arrondissement.* You can get it at a news kiosk or any bookstore. The small, fat, red book or the thinner, larger, black edition give you detailed maps of each arrondissement, including every alley, dead end, and passageway in town. On the page preceding each of these maps is a list of the important buildings or sites, museums, hospitals, churches, police stations, post offices, and the days the outdoor markets, or *marchés,* are open. The street directory (in alphabetical order) lists the arrondissement, the section of the map, the streets that lie at either end of your street, the numbers of the corner buildings of those streets, and the closest métro stop. A métro map and schematic drawings of the bus routes are also included.

RESTAURANTS

Restaurant-going in Paris is a fine art, and entire books are devoted to the subject. Restaurants serve lunch from 12 or 12:30 until about 2:30. Dinner is never served before seven, and the fancier the restaurant, the later it fills. (Don't go before eight to a gourmet restaurant, and 8:30 or 9 p.m. is better.) Meals are often copious, comprising at least three courses, sometimes as many as seven. Take your time and make it an evening—never expect to eat an expensive meal before going to the movies. The chef and your stomach expect you to give the food the same attention it got when it was prepared.

Knowing how to order and what to expect is often difficult. In this regard it is a wise idea to check the menu and prices posted, by law, outside the restaurant. This may save you from surprises and embarrassment. (Beauty salons and barber shops are also required to post prices.) The set-price *(prix fixe)* menu or the *spécialité de la maison* are a good idea. The first will almost always be well balanced and economical. The owners are not palming anything off on you but rather trying to pass on to you the savings that they made on a special purchase. The same is true of a *spécialité.* It may be the chef's regional culinary masterpiece or it may be the spring lamb that he was able to obtain for the first time of the year just that morning. Don't be afraid to ask what something is or what the *maître d'hôtel* would recommend. If you take his advice, he will be flattered, and your service will be even more careful. This is particularly true of the better restaurants. The same advice goes for the wine steward *(sommelier).* Unless you know your wines well and you are already paying a substantial sum for an exquisite meal, don't worry over the wine list. Tell the *sommelier* what you're eating and in what price range you'd like to drink, and let him pick. If you are in a cheaper restaurant eating a standard French meal (already far superior to what you get for twice the price in the

United States) and you're not fussy, you can ask for a pitcher of house wine. A *carafe* is a liter; a *demie* is a half liter; and a *quart* is a quarter. If you don't like wine, or you find that you fall asleep for two hours in the afternoon when you imbibe at lunch, stick to the mineral waters, naturally bubbly Perrier or plain sweet water like Evian, Vittel, or Contrexeville. The French depend on bottled water to ease their digestion and keep their weight down. (It is difficult to judge the truth of these claims. Half of our French friends are trim and eat with pleasure, the other half have the famous French malady, liver trouble, *mal au foie.*) Whatever you choose to drink at lunch, don't ask for milk. The waiter would be undone, and even if you did convince him to get it for you, you might be surprised at its unhomogenized and slightly acid taste.

Another thing to avoid is strong drink (distilled liquor) before dinner; it dulls your tastebuds, as does smoking at table, which can also bother the other diners. (Some of France's great chefs have been known to ban guests so indifferent to fine cuisine as to smoke during the meal.) The French drink an apéritif before dinner; we recommend a kir, a combination of dry white wine and crème de cassis.

You will be given bread in a restaurant but usually no butter, except with certain foods such as oysters (served with rye bread and butter) or radishes. If you really want it, ask for it. The bread is made for soaking up sauces, and it is not considered crude to break off a piece, spear it with a fork, and mop up your salad dressing. You may begin the meal with tomatoes, cucumbers, or red cabbage, but lettuce salad is always served after the meat course; it is not mixed with any other vegetables and is served with an oil and vinegar dressing. When you order a steak *(entrecôte, bifteck, tournedos,* or *filet mignon)* in France don't ask for it well done *(bien cuit).* You won't get it that way, and the chef will feel pleased he's saving you from your bad eating habits. *Saignant* means rare, that is, bluish, and *à point* (literally, just right) is the reddish-pink color Americans usually associate with rare meat. That is as far as you'll get in a good restaurant (unless you're prepared to send your meat back once or twice). If you're in a cheaper one and you get well-done meat, you can be sure that it will be too tough to chew. If you can't handle rare meat, skip the beef and eat lamb or veal, which is particularly excellent in France.

If you order a *café* after your meal, you will get a very strong demitasse of black coffee. The French never put milk in their coffee once they've had their *café au lait* at breakfast; cream in your coffee after dinner is therefore considered a strange request. If French coffee keeps you awake, ask for the decaffeinated coffee that is now served in most restaurants.

Sitting at a sidewalk café is a perfect pleasure in Paris. They are everywhere and of every sort. The cafés on the big streets are best for people-watching, but a cup of coffee may cost a dollar or more. Remember that you are really paying for your chair, and if you choose, you can sit in most cafés with your one cup of coffee for three hours or all day and read, write, watch, and feel French. (We wouldn't recommend this, though, at the heavy-traffic, high-turnover places. They expect you to order a new drink every so often, especially at busy times.) The small, dark, corner café is the local hangout. The customers know the owner; there is frequently a pinball machine *(flipper)* with a few men sitting around and gossiping. They will eye you suspiciously as you enter, but in a few days you too can become a "regular" if you wish to. Drinks are cheaper standing at the bar than at the tables, but remember there to leave a small tip for service. At the tables it is almost always included in the bill. Almost every café will serve some food, ranging from breakfast croissants through sandwiches *(casse-croûtes)* to omelets and simple meat meals. There are usually no menus but signs are posted on the walls. We feel, however, that other than breakfast, café food is not a very wise expenditure; the sandwiches are too bready, the meat too tough.

A red cigar-shaped sign over the door of a café designates it as a *tabac*, which means you can buy cigarettes, matches, and stamps at the counter, and mail your letter in the pale yellow post box right outside the door. Cafés are important for another reason; they almost always have restrooms. A nice café should have decent toilets, or WCs (water closets). In the corner café you run the risk of finding a Turkish toilet, an acceptable invention for men but an obstacle course for women. A Turkish toilet consists of a hole in the center of a square porcelain area in the floor with two footprints at the front. In a Turkish toilet you probably won't even find the wax paper that French have traditionally used as toilet tissue. It helps to carry some Kleenex.

TIPPING

Here is a list of how much to tip around Paris. First, never let yourself be forced into more than you want to give. If you get bad service, respond in kind. The French are trying to deny it, but the dumb, wealthy American and the timid poorer one are relics of the past. Because travelers are wiser and more careful with their money these days, most restaurants, cafés, and hotels place an automatic 15 percent service charge on the bill. If you have any doubts about whether or not your bill includes service, ask, *"Service compris?"* If the service is included, you may round out your change, but this is not compulsory.

Taxis—10 to 15 percent
Washroom attendants—20 to 50 centimes
Waiters—12 to 15 percent if the service is not already included
Wine steward—2 to 5 francs, depending on the quality of the wine and the restaurant
Cafés—12 to 15 percent at the counter; service is included at the table
Cloakroom attendants—50 centimes to 1 franc per person
Museum guides—1 franc, as you leave
Park chairs—if requested, about 50 centimes
Porters—1 franc per piece of luggage
Hairdressers—10 to 20 percent plus 1 or 2 francs for the assistant
Theater and movie ushers—20 to 50 centimes in a cheap movie, 1 to 2 francs per group in a theater

TELEPHONES

This brings us to the telephone. First, use your hotel desk or room phone whenever possible. If forced out into the complicated world, you should know that the equivalent of a dime will be of no use. You must buy—in a métro, a café, a restaurant, or the post office a token, *jeton,* to use in a pay phone. A *jeton* costs 50-65 centimes. (The post office *jetons* are different from those used in cafés and restaurants; they also cost slightly less.) Fortunately, you will find phones where you find *jetons,* but you will not see outdoor boxes as at home or in England—surprising in a country where the rate of vandalism is so low. Often the phone booth in a café or restaurant will be down some steep, narrow stairs. Pick up the receiver, put in your token, wait for a dial tone, then dial your number. When the party at the other end answers—and only then—push the button that is marked *pour parler appuyez* (push to talk), or the party will not be able to hear your voice. Pushing the button means that your *jeton* has been swallowed and you will never see it again, so be sure to wait for a response at the other end before pushing the button.

If you want to reach someone in Paris and the telephone defies you, or if your friend has no phone, send a message by pneumatic tube (called a *pneumatique*) at the post office. Buy a *pneumatique* letter for three francs, write your message, and mail it in a slot marked *pneumatiques.* Your letter will zoom under the Paris streets through the sewer system and arrive at the post office nearest its destination, from which point it will be delivered, fresh as a daisy, two hours later.

SHOPPING

Be brave and buy that French dress or suit you have always wanted. With luck, you'll love what you buy and wear it forever with pleasure. We do, however, have a few warning words. Prices are high, but so are they at home. Salespeople have been known to expect you to buy the first thing you try on. Simply let them understand you'll make up your own mind, thank you. Don't allow yourself to make an unwilling purchase.

On the next page we have listed a size chart for men and women. When in doubt, try the larger size. The French tend to be smaller and thinner than Americans.

If you're determined to buy French clothes but can't seem to cope with the shop assistants, try the large department stores where you will remain anonymous. We recommend Au Printemps or the Galeries Lafayettes. These stores carry everything and are located right behind American Express at the Chaussée d'Antin métro stop. If you make a large purchase ($20 in most stores, though some randomly decide their minimum), and you have your passport with you, you can buy the item tax free. All the Common Market countries have a sales tax already included in the price of the goods—a tax that tourists don't have to pay. Ask the cashier about the TVA (tax to value added), and if you are buying enough, they will fill out a customs form and give you an addressed envelope for their store. When you arrive at French customs at the airport or the border you must give them the forms and show them your purchase. Be sure to pack it on top. They will then stamp everything, and a few weeks later your money will be refunded by mail. Be sure to arrive at the airport with enough time to do this; you won't be alone at the customs desk.

Despite the current wave of inflation some good buys you

Women's Sizes

DRESSES

United States	Great Britain	France
8	10	38
10	12	40
12	14	42
14	16	44
16	18	46
18	20	48

SWEATERS, BLOUSES

United States	Great Britain	France
10	32	38
12	34	40
14	36	42
16	38	44
18	40	46
20	42	48

SHOES

United States	Great Britain	France
4½	3	35½
5	3½	36
5½	4	36½
6	4½	37
6½	5	37½
7	5½	38
7½	6	38½
8	6½	39
8½	7	39½

Men's Sizes

SUITS

United States and Great Britain	France
34	34
35	36
36	38
37	40
38	42
39	44
40	46
42	48

SHIRTS

United States and Great Britain	France
14	35
14+	36
14½	37
15	38
15+	39
15½	40
16	41
16½	42
17	43
17+	44

SHOES

United States	Great Britain	France
6½	6	39
7½	7	40
8	7½	41
8½	8	42
9½	9	43
10½	10	44
11	10½	45
12	11½	46
12½	12	47

can still take advantage of in France are: shoes, Bally and Charles Jourdan; socks and stockings, Dim in particular; French notebooks and date books; leather books, wallets, and brief-cases; and anything from a Prisunic, Monoprix, Uniprix, or the other five-and-dime type stores all over France. If you're not trying to save money, have fun—look in the boutiques and department stores like Frank and Fils (women) at Métro La Muette and Jones (men and women) on the Ave. Victor Hugo.

Food shopping in Paris is a pleasure, but there are certain rules to follow: First, never expect the prices to be less than at home; they are usually higher. Whereas Americans spend something like 12 percent of their salaries on food, the French spend 40 percent. Second, never touch the fruit or vegetables unless no one is looking. That is a cardinal sin. If you're not in Paris long enough to get to know the merchants, you just have to take a chance on getting good produce. Third, carry your own shopping bag. If you are in a delicatessen (*charcuterie*) and buy runny salads, ask for plastic bags. About the *charcuterie*—the food is usually as good as it looks. The best way to lunch in Paris is to buy cold meats and salads from the *charcuterie*, cheese from the dairy store (*crèmerie*), bread from the bakery (*boulangerie*), and wine from the wine merchant (*marchand de vins*), and make a messy, joyful picnic in your hotel room or on the nearest park bench. (The grass is almost always forbidden, *interdit*.) There are also little groceries (labeled *alimentation générale*) where you can buy all of these and more. But their standards are not those of the specialty shops, and they are not less expensive. They do save walking, but why would you want to do that? **Don't forget knives, forks, plates, napkins, cups, and a corkscrew from home!** For maximum pleasure and economy, never travel without this equipment. Fourth, avoid American products. Tropicana orange juice, for example, is at least a dollar a liter (a bit less than a quart), and Coca Cola is the same price as wine. (Most bottles are returnable so don't throw them away.) Five, French bread has no preservatives and will not be edible the next day or even that night if you buy it in the morning. The price of that fantastic bread is regulated by the government, so standard breads cost the same everywhere. The price of fancy breads like wood-fire, whole wheat, or viennoise, a soft white bread, will vary—as do the prices of pastries, from shop to shop—but only slightly. Six, food stores are open from 8 or 9 a.m. to 1-1:30, then closed until four or five o'clock, and then open again in the evening until 7 or 8 p.m. You can starve in Paris looking for food in the intervening afternoon hours. Try the Drugstores (high prices) or stores like Monoprix and Prisunic (lower prices) if you're in trouble. Most shops are also closed on Mondays, except for the grocery chain of Felix Potin. In August the problem of closed shops and restaurants will be greatly aggravated, as is the difficulty of finding medical help. No self-respecting Frenchman would be caught dead in Paris that month, just when all the tourists are there. Indeed, late spring and early fall are the best times to visit.

WHAT'S HAPPENING

The best way to find out what's going on is *This Week in Paris (La Semaine de Paris)*, sold at any newsstand. It comes out in French and English versions and gives you all the information on plays, exhibits, tours, concerts, museums, lectures, movies, restaurants, strip shows, cabarets, TV programs, and everything else happening in Paris and the suburbs, with the dates, hours, and prices. Movies are almost always subtitled, not dubbed; there are student rates except Saturday and Sunday, and you must tip the girl who seats you 20-50 centimes (slightly more for opera or theater).

HELP

There are various kinds of help that you may need in Paris. In a medical emergency call the American Hospital of Paris at 63 Blvd. Victor Hugo, Neuilly, telephone 637-72-00. The staff speak English, and many of the doctors are American or American-trained. If you intend to remain in Paris for a long time, you may wish to get an identification card from the hospital and carry it with you in case of accident. Or make your own. Simply state your name, address, that you are an American, and in case of accident you wish to be taken to the American Hospital.

If you are too sick to get to the hospital, call a French doctor. They make the almost unheard-of house call as a matter of course. Ask a French friend, the American Hospital, or your local pharmacy for the name of a doctor. There is no guarantee, of course, that you will be able to communicate with him when he comes. Also available are SOS doctors at 707-77-77. These are doctors in radio-controlled cars with medical and pharmaceutical equipment. This service is available only at night, Sundays, and on holidays.

For common minor problems, like an upset stomach, pharmacies in France give simple medical advice if you are only slightly ill. Beware, however, of their recommendations; a French idiosyncrasy is the use of suppositories, not pills, and you may find out too late that your headache remedy is not in swallowable form. You may want to bring your favorite American remedy from home.

The following is a list of pharmacies that are open at odd hours:

RIGHT BANK

Les Drugstores, 133 Avenue des Champs Elysées, 8e, and Rond Point des Champs Elysées, both open 8:30-2 a.m.

Pharmacie Proniewski, 5 Place Blanche, 9e, always open, except Sunday 9 a.m.-8 p.m., Monday 9 a.m.-12 noon

Pharmacie Caron, 24 Rue de la Paix, 2e, daily 8 a.m.-12:30 a.m., Sunday and Monday 7:30 p.m.-11:30 p.m.

Pharmacie de la Muette, 11 Chaussée de la Muette, 16e, daily 8:30 a.m.-11:30 p.m., Monday 12 p.m.-11:30 p.m., closed Sunday

LEFT BANK

Le Drugstore, 149 Blvd. St. Germain, 6e, daily 8:30 a.m.-2:00 a.m.

Pharmacie des Arts, 106 Blvd. Montparnasse, 14e, daily 8:00 a.m.-1:00 a.m.

Pharmacie Hughes, 315 Avenue Vaugirard, 15e, daily 9 a.m.-12 a.m., Monday 12 p.m.-12 a.m.

If your local pharmacy is closed, the name of the closest open one will be posted on his door.

If you have lost your passport or are in some trouble, the American embassy is at the northwest corner of the Place de la Concorde. There are also certain tourist centers in Paris where English is spoken and information is given:

Automobile Association of America, 9 Rue de la Paix, 073-35-08

Commissariat Générale de Tourisme, 8 Avenue de l'Opéra, 742-11-39

Bureau National de Tourisme, 127 Avenue des Champs
  Elysées, 225-12-80
Air Terminal des Invalides, Esplanade des Invalides, 7e,
  705-82-81
Gare du Nord, Rue de Dunkerque, 10e, LAM-77-28
Gare de l'Est, Place de Strasbourg, 10e, BOT-49-90

If you become very homesick for an American tuna salad
sandwich, coke, and honest-to-goodness American ice cream, go
to the American Center on the Rue du Dragon, 6e, right off
Blvd. St. Germain. They have a cafeteria downstairs, as well as a
listening room with a fine collection of American records, a
gallery, a small library of American books, and lectures,
concerts, plays, and movies—mostly for free. We saw *Easy Rider,
The Importance of Being Earnest,* and heard Gloria Steinem, among
others, on our visits there.

If you are a student and would like to make contact with other
American students go to Reid Hall at 4 Rue de Chevreuse, 6e.
This is a residence owned by Columbia University and affiliated
with other colleges and universities as well. They have a dining
room open to anyone where you can get a cheap, good meal in an
atmosphere similar to that of an American college dining
commons.

St. Julien le Pauvre

METRO: St. Michel, Maubert Mutualité

BUS: No. 24, 27, 47, 63, 86, 87

STREETS: Place du Petit Pont, Rue du Petit Pont, Blvd. St. Jacques, Rue de la Bûcherie, Rue St. Julien le Pauvre, Rue du Fouarre, Rue Galande, Rue de l'Hôtel Colbert, Rue Frédéric Sauton, Impasse Maubert, Rue Maître Albert, Quai de Montebello

STARTING POINT: The corner of the Petit Pont and the Quai de Montebello

> *Boil three hundred slugs, skim off the grease, add three tablespoons of olive oil and one tablespoon of honey and anoint your skull with the mixture.*
>
> > —*Recipe to cure baldness given by André Fournier,*
> > *professor at the School of Medicine in 1540.*

Here you are in the heart of Paris, looking at Notre Dame on the Ile de la Cité, where the Parisii, a tribe for whom the city is named, originally settled, long before Caesar came here in 50 B.C. At that time there were eight or nine islands in this region of the Seine; now there are only two—this one and, behind it, the Ile St. Louis.

The *parvis,* the square in front of Notre Dame, is the official center of France, the spot from which every distance in the nation is measured. The stone markers you see along the French roadside count the kilometers to the *parvis* of Notre Dame. Today's walk will not take you farther than 0 kilometers Paris, but there is much to see.

The Seine in prehistoric times was a wide, slow-flowing river over 100 feet higher than it is today. The river meandered all over the area between Mont-Ste-Geneviève to the south (take a look about five blocks down and you will see a hill) and Montmartre, one whole mile away to the north. (You are now looking at less than one half the present channel—the distance from the island to the quai. The other, larger half lies between the island and the Right Bank.)

Even Parisians forget the river was so wide, but in 1910 an

extraordinary flood in the month of January reminded them of the tributaries of the Seine still flowing underground. At that time these subterranean waters welled to the surface and over the banks. From the present course of the river to the Place de l'Opéra and the Gare St. Lazare to the suburbs of the north, the secret Seine came up from hiding and took possession of the city once again.

Postcards picturing the flood show men and women rowing around Paris at the level of shop signs. A great many important historical records were lost, including those of some of the major libraries and banks of the city. Deep cellars in this area are still cemented in mud from the flood, and excavations constantly unearth buried architecture and artifacts.

For ancient Paris this sprawling river, whose waters were sweet and clean enough to drink, was a boon. Because of it, the Parisii felt safe from surprise attacks; an enemy would have to cross large stretches of swamp to reach the island. The river was also an excellent highway for trade, as it still is today. By Gallic times the Seine had already dug its present channel, but the banks to either side, especially the Right Bank, remained swampy and uninhabitable. The first part of the mainland to be settled was the south or Left Bank, where the ground rose more sharply than on the marshy Right Bank (which was aptly called the Marais, or swamp). If you look up the Rue du Petit Pont with your back to the bridge, you will see, about 200 yards away, beyond what is now the Rue des Ecoles, the College of France on the left side and the observatory tower of the Sorbonne on the right. Two thousand years ago Roman baths stood on these sites—the Romans occupied Gaul, including Paris, for over 400 years—for it was on this hill that the ancient residents finally got far enough above the water line to build important structures. The remains of the baths still exist under the College of France; other ruins close by, unearthed as recently as 1946, can be seen in the garden of the Cluny Museum. The area between this high water line and the river, the area you are visiting today, was settled much later.

The site of the present church of St. Séverin, the back of which you can see down the Rue du Petit Pont on the right, was a small dry ground swell where a hermit chose to settle in the fifth century. Later, as the Seine continued to dig itself a deeper channel, the area between high ground and the river was filled in with houses and narrow paths.

Even during the Middle Ages the street level was 30 feet, two stories, lower than it is today. Notice the 30 feet of dikes that rise from the Seine. Where that dike stands, houses once stood: Until the middle of the nineteenth century the streets and alleys of the *quartier* ran steeply down to the river's edge. This is the reason three levels of cellar still exist in the seventeenth-century buildings you see on the Left Bank quais. The present ground-floor stores (the café, Le Notre Dame, and Optique, for example) are on what was once the second floor of these buildings.

The first bridge connecting the Ile de la Cité to its banks, the present Petit Pont, was built here because at this point the island is closest to the Left Bank. A little fortress, Le Petit Châtelet, which doubled as toll house, stood at the end of the bridge, on the spot where you are now. It was the custom then, as it is today on bridges and highways, to pay a toll in order to pass in and out of the city. Another larger fortress, the 'Grand Châtelet, stood on the Right Bank at the Pont St. Michel. Both these bastions were used as prisons during the French Revolution. With the help of underground passageways to many points in the vicinity, prison affairs could easily be disposed of under ground.

The Petit Pont was not only a passageway; two- and three-story houses and shops lined either side, making it the busiest street in town. In the Middle Ages the picturesque aspect of this bridge, really a street thrown across the river, was enlivened by philosophers offering their intellectual wares, by jugglers, singers, and dog and bear trainers. During the day it was a paradise for cutpurses, at night for cutthroats.

This bridge has been rebuilt because of fire and flood and attacks more times than the French care to count. Fire was the most common cause of destruction until the eighteenth century, when the bridge was finally rebuilt in stone.

Here is one version of a story that has been told about the bridge and its famous fires. The people of the Middle Ages believed that bodies drowned in the Seine could be located by setting afloat in the river a votive candle on a wooden disk and noting where it stopped or went out. It was doubly important to find drowned bodies because a huge fee of 101 *écus*, the equivalent of a year's pay for a manual laborer, is said to have been charged for the delivery of a loved one from the morgue at the Châtelet.

Rue de la Bûcherie, opposite Notre Dame

There was once a poor old widow whose son had drowned, and she set a candle afloat hoping to find his body. The candle floated close to a straw-laden barge, setting it afire. The barge in turn went into the wooden scaffolding of a pillar of the bridge. From there the flames spread onto the bridge itself and, after three days of raging fire, destroyed the bridge and the houses on it. Beautiful and detailed engravings of the history of the Petit Pont, before, during, and after the fire, hang in the sitting room of the Hôtel Mt. Blanc on the Rue de la Huchette (see Walk 2). The proprietor will be pleased to show them to you.

If you'd like to, climb down the steps on the Right Bank near the Petit Pont or on the Left Bank toward the Pont au Double, and look at the Seine up close. You will be in the company of fishermen who catch live, though small, fish, of *clochards,* bums who find this spot slightly warmer and more private for sleeping than the streets, and of lovers of all ages expressing various degrees of affection.

The Quai de Montebello, the street that runs along the

riverside in front of you and is packed with cars (we say this with absolute confidence after having watched the street over an entire year at all hours of the day and night) was built by Baron Georges Haussmann. He was the famous city planner of Napoleon III (in the 1850s and 1860s) who built most of the avenues and boulevards that have fortunately and unfortunately saved Paris for the automobile.

Cross the quai with the light. (Watch for turning cars.) The small green strip of park before you was once covered by the Petit Châtelet; later, there was an annex of the Hôtel Dieu hospital here. The park was finally cleared only about 50 years ago. This little park with benches and *boules* (or bowls) players and the park of St. Julien le Pauvre to your left (with your back to the river) are the only pieces of green on the Left Bank of Paris—the only spots as far down as the Eiffel Tower that the French have allowed to lie fallow instead of being covered with apartments or industry. This vest-pocket park belongs to vagrants, who stretch out full length and sleep on their rolled-up belongings for a pillow, and to the *boules* players who meet at lunchtime or before dinner.

One day we were in the park with our grandson and nephew, aged one, who was intently pulling on his bottle of milk, when one of the *clochards* spotted him. The bum jumped up from his semistupor, seized his bottle of wine, threw his head back, and started guzzling in imitation, laughing and hopping about all the while. He sobered for a moment, stared hard at the baby, and in a great bond of friendship counseled him, "*Mon petit*, keep it up for the rest of your life."

PLACE DU PETIT PONT

The street that leads out from the bridge is called the Place du Petit Pont. At the next crossing it changes its name to the Rue du Petit Pont. In both places, the street is the same width. If you look very hard at the buildings on either side of the Rue du Petit Pont, you will probably be able to figure out why. The apartment houses on the left side of the street were built in the seventeenth century; they are straight buildings with slim rectangular windows, free of ornamentation except for the iron grillwork on the windows. Across the street nineteenth-century buildings, heavy with curves, carvings, protuberances, and balconies, stand on ground cleared when the street was widened and rebuilt 200 years later, in 1857.

The Rue du Petit Pont lasts one short block, when for no

visible reason it becomes the Rue St. Jacques. From prehistoric times this road, which climbs straight up the gentle hill in front of you, was the main road from Paris to the south. When the Romans first came to Lutèce, which was what Paris was then called, they came this way. Soon thereafter they transformed the dirt road into a 9-meter (30 feet)-wide stone highway. Two huge stones from this construction were found in 1926 below the ground surface. You will see them later in the *parvis* of St. Julien le Pauvre. Elephant remains have also turned up, which gives you an idea of how the Romans thought big and were able to build big, and why we still speak in admiration and awe of Roman roads.

As early as 1230 the Rue St. Jacques was given its present name because the famous pilgrimage to the shrine of St. James (St. Jacques) of Compostella traveled south along this road. Santiago (Spanish for St. James) de Compostella, a city on the Atlantic coast of Spain, was rich in scallop shells, *coquilles,* which the pilgrims were quick to gather and bring back as proof of their voyage and their devotion. They exposed the shells whenever and wherever possible, and as a result we still eat *coquilles* St. Jacques. Their actions also explain the use of shell designs in stone on buildings and churches and in wood on furniture.

RUE DE LA BUCHERIE

Return to the Rue de la Bûcherie, the street facing the small park, pass the café on the corner, and stop at the restaurant, the **Bûcherie.** *Bûcherie* means a storehouse for wood. It was on this street that barges loaded with logs for houses and heating deposited their goods. The name of the street, as is often the case in Paris, reflected its activity. This restaurant remembers its past, not only in its name, but with a wood fire, which burns continuously on a hearth in the center of the room. It was, and still is, a hangout for actors and politicians, though the celebrities themselves change. The restaurant is not inexpensive. A full dinner here might include the specialty of the house, which is an odd but delicious dish. The order of arrangement, if you can believe it, is as follows, starting from the bottom up: unsweetened crust, cooked sliced apples, tender beef fillet, slice of pâté de foie gras, mushrooms, and all of it capped with a rosy cream sauce. Recipe on p. 167. Even if you choose not to dine here, peer in the windows to look at the back wall. It is covered with a tapestry woven for the restaurant by the most famous contemporary tapestry maker, the reviver of an ancient art, Lurçat. He used to live upstairs and wove this wall of tapestry as a gift.

No. 39. The house next door is most amazing. The houses we have been looking at are mostly seventeenth century; this one was built in the early sixteenth. It is a small two-story wooden structure, the kind that was typical 500 years ago and can still be seen in towns like York in England, Riquewihr in Alsace, or Conques in southern France, but has almost vanished from most European cities. The building once served as an inn and was hidden from sight for most of its long history. The Petit Châtelet, as the inn was called—after the fortress it stood behind and to whose employees it gave meat and drink over the centuries—was tucked away until 1909, when the ground was cleared between the Rue de la Bûcherie and the river. What a shame the building is unoccupied and the tavern permanently closed.

The little building is architecturally interesting for several reasons. Almost no wooden structures in Paris have survived; the big enemy has been fire, as evidenced from the history of the Petit Pont. Note the large dormer windows that jut out from the steep roof line and the smaller windows on the attic floor above. Look at the exposed side of the building on the right, and you will see coming out from the exterior wall the ends of the framing beams used in its construction some hundreds of years ago. These are the wooden joists we sometimes see as exposed rafters in a ceiling.

Now look at the exposed side of the building on the left. There you will see one of the only three open staircases, *escaliers à claire voie,* left in Paris. This was the typical staircase of the sixteenth century, replaced in the seventeenth by the closed *escalier à vis.* We will wind up and down several of these corkscrew staircases in today's walk.

Immediately to the left is **Shakespeare and Co.** This is the oddest bookstore we have ever been in. George Whitman, the owner (and a cousin of Walt), doesn't try very hard to sell books; he just likes people who like to read. The ground floor is mainly devoted to books-for-sale of all kinds—old, new, mostly in English, and in no particular order that we could see. You can browse in corners, on chairs, or on the floor.

Up some very narrow stairs is Whitman's own library. Here the walls are covered with books he does not sell, and here is where one gets the feeling of Whitman's unusual personality. If you nose around long enough and look interested, Whitman will invite you to tea. Here you can read his books in floppy chairs or on a big bed (reputed to have a few fleas), meet people, even take a nap if you wish. Don't be offended if Whitman seems to ignore you; despite his great hospitality he is a man of very few words and many moods. But the atmosphere remains friendly and relaxed.

More than a bookseller, Whitman takes in travelers, if he has room, and gives them a bed, provided they follow the rules of the house: Work a few hours a day in the store; read a book a night.

Running a bookstore this way has its trials. Whitman was forbidden by the French government to sell books for a period of two years. The reason given for this prohibition was that he was a foreigner, hence could not own and operate a business in France. He did have a French partner, but the government claimed that this was in name only and tried to close the shop down. For two years, then, Whitman tried to survive on "voluntary" contributions based on the value of the books taken by "visitors." Finally, and no doubt in desperation, Whitman became a French citizen.

We suspect that the real reason he had difficulties with the authorities had nothing to do with nationality but rather with the fact that his store is a haven for the homeless, footloose, and, by official standards, potentially undesirable. In France, where a certificate of residency is all important, it isn't hard to imagine the excitement and irritation at the Prefecture of Police right across the river, when 50 or more young people, most of them with long hair and strange dress, gave Shakespeare and Co. as their address.

Shakespeare and Co. has always promoted the literary avant garde. When the bookstore was originally founded by Sylvia Beach, it was the only house that would publish James Joyce's *Ulysses*. Now Whitman gives young writers a chance to be heard at poetry readings (in his library every Monday night at eight) and to be published in his review.

Give this store some browsing time. It is generally open from 12 to 12, or 1 to 1. If you want a souvenir of Paris, buy a book and get it stamped here. The inscription around the head of William reads, "Shakespeare and Co. Kilometer Zero Paris."

RUE ST. JULIEN LE PAUVRE

Now let us go around the corner into the Rue St. Julien le Pauvre and look at the seventeenth-century houses across the street from the park. Notice the cleaned soft-beige stone building, **No. 10**, and, in particular, the elegant windows of the first-floor apartment, which are taller than all the others. If you count the panes on each story you will see that the number of panes goes down and the windows get smaller as you go up. At the very top the tiny mansard windows (named for its inventor, the architect François Mansard), which peep out from the sloping roof, are reduced to one small pane of glass. The taller windows of the first floor mean, of course, higher ceilings, a mark of distinction still dear to the French, especially in old, nonstandardized apartments.

The exterior decoration tells the same story. Thus, the iron railings on the protruding sills of the two balconies on this first floor are finer than those on the floor above, after which there are no more balconies or grillwork at all. Look at other examples of this art of handwrought iron decoration on nineteenth-century houses as well as those of the seventeenth century as you walk around the city.

It is clear that the first floor above the street was once the coveted apartment (*appartement noble*), and it is from this point the French begin to number their floors. If that living ro m behind the tall windows were yours, you would say you lived on the first floor (*premier étage*), not the second floor of the building. The ground floor, called the *rez de chausée,* which means "even with the road," was and still is reserved for the concierge's one or two rooms, the courtyards, and the trash. The wealthy nobles and bankers stepped up one flight, the middle-class profession-als and shopkeepers climbed two or three, while the servants and workers trudged to the top. Each apartment building, therefore, in all but the poorest neighborhoods, contained a microcosm of French society.

The advent of the elevator, however, turned this arrange-ment upside down and made possible the one-class high-rise building. Today the servants' rooms—often used as workshops or extra bedrooms, for sleep-in servants are hard to come by— are located on the ground floor; the apartments cost more the higher you go; and the prize residence is a sunlit, glass-enclosed, terraced retreat at the top, as far as possible from the city's noise and dirt. There are relatively few of these newer apartment buildings on the Left Bank, but the next time you visit the bourgeois neighborhoods of western Paris—the eighth, sixteenth, or seventeenth arrondissements—take a look at the imposing, prosperous buildings with their cut-stone facades, and follow the lines of balconies up to the elegant penthouses at the top.

Nos. 4 to 8 on your right are all owned by the same people. The **Esmeralda Hotel**, No. 4, has a charming entry, filled with fresh flowers and country furniture, plus an authentic and richly raftered ceiling. Go in and look. We do not, however, recommend the hotel. The man at the desk showed us a picture-book room, which we promptly reserved for friends. That's the showpiece. When the weary travelers arrived, they were given a room so small they had to climb over the bed to get into the bathroom. The price, however, remained substantial.

No. 6. The top half of each window of the Restaurant Esmeralda is caged behind thick vertical bars of iron, which once served as protection against thieves. The bottom half was removable, and is therefore now gone, the top half stationary and still in place. (The practice of fixing iron grills or curtains over storefronts goes back centuries in France but has now fallen into disuse, especially in good neighborhoods. The sight of these forbidding barriers used to shock Americans, who had never seen their like. They do not shock any longer. We seem to have picked up where the French left off: Our shopkeepers no longer feel secure; theirs do.) Look above the restaurant now at the building on top, and you will be surprised at its narrowness; there is only enough room for one window per floor. Notice the double window up top under the gabled roof.

The restaurant has been artfully restored with exposed rafters, rustic furniture, and walls covered with paintings. The prices are reasonable; try their stuffed omelets, pepper steak, or grilled meat. The young people who serve here are helpful and pleasant.

No. 8 is simply called Esmeralda and is a narrow shop—semi-antique, semijunk. Old Clothes, lace blouses, and uniforms of all sorts fill the racks on the left; the right side of the store is piled with bits of jewelry, doll furniture, and cups and plates less than 20 years old. Bargains are scarce but not unfindable. The shop is open from 2 to 10 p.m.

No. 10. Satay is an ultrasleek restaurant with shiny cocoa-

Doorway of No. 14, Rue St. Julien le Pauvre

colored walls and jute on the floor, all of which goes together very well with the warm old beige stones and dark heavy rafters. The spacious armchairs around small low tables invite you to a quiet and private dinner. Although the menu looks exotic, with dishes from the Far East and creative cocktails with names like The Leopard and The Dutchman, the restaurant still smells as if good French cooking were going on. Reasonable price for dinner, which is the only meal served; the Satay opens at 6 p.m.

No. 12. L'Arbre Vert is an odd place on this street of tourist offerings. Primarily an institute of psychotherapy, but an art gallery as well, it lends an air of mystery and meditation to the neighborhood. This pleases the average residents, who take pride in their offbeat neighbors, just as they do in the artists, writers, and architects who choose to live here because they draw inspiration from old Paris.

The small office you see gives no hint of the imposing titles and activities of the tenants: L'Arbre Vert is the seat of the National Syndicate of Psychotherapists and the International Society for the Method of Mental Imagery. A modern spiral staircase leads to two subcellars where classes (part of a 3-year course) are given to students and doctors. M. André Virel, the guru director, believes that the analysis of dreams with emphasis on mental imagery can be used in the cure and treatment of personality disorders. The mental image implied in the institute's name, a tree forever green, not only suggests human growth but refers specifically to the oldest tree in Paris, which continues to bloom every spring in the garden across the street.

A very important person lives in the house above: the architect, Claude Frémin, who is responsible for some of the most remarkable restorations in the area—this house at No. 12 and the Auberge des Deux Signes around the corner on the Rue Galande. We'll be getting there later.

Next door at **No. 14** we come to an impressive old stone gateway with massive wooden doors. Look above at the pediment where Themis, the Greek goddess of "justice in all its relations to men," sits. She is represented as a dignified and commanding prophetess holding the scales that balance justice, surrounded by olive branches of peace, while a cherub holds an hourglass. The symbolism of this sculpture was carefully chosen, for in the early seventeenth century this was the official residence of Isaac Lafférmas, Prefect of Police of the

Châtelet under Cardinal Richelieu. The prefect was, among other things, the king's executioner, and we have cause to wonder how wisely he used those scales. While he and his family lived comfortably above ground, three levels of cellars below were used as a prison. (The cellars date from the fourteenth century and were originally used to house the monks from the church of St. Julien le Pauvre across the street.) This prison eventually fell into disuse in the seventeenth century, but 150 years later, in 1793, the Revolution created such an overflow of prisoners in the Petit and Grand Châtelets, and everywhere else, that these cells were restored to use. We have it on firsthand information that instruments of torture, real ones, rusted ones, still exist in the lowest basement. Hélène, an excellent hairdresser and good friend to many in the *quartier*, whose salon is just down the street, saw them with her own eyes when she and her husband were on the track of a damaged water pipe. There is a rack down there and a devilish seat with a hole in it to allow the heat from boiling oil below to cook the bound and helpless victim. All this in the name of justice.

Walk through the wide entrance into the handsome square courtyard. To your right, facing the entrance to the house, you will find a modern doorway, an unbroken sheath of plate glass, through which you can see the elegant old curved iron stair rail, wood carving on the wall to your left, and a wormeaten and nail-holed timber above the doorway to the left of that. Notice how some sections of the wall are free of plaster. This is done to expose the stonework and show the walls as they looked originally. The French call this *pierre apparente*, visible stone. The practice of plastering all interior surfaces was introduced in the seventeenth century as a precaution against fire. It was not the stone that was flammable, but the exposed beam ends were. Peer sharply to your right and you will see a plaque commemorating Isaac Laffémas and the fact that he lived and served his king here.

This entrance, glassed in only 20 years ago, represents the perfect blending of the old and new, and is typical of the tasteful restoration that goes on all over this neighborhood.

Look up at this magnificent building, and note in particular the stone moldings that surround each stately window. They almost resemble shutters, though real shutters did not come into use until a later date. The roof is spotted with tall gabled windows. Rumor has it that the baron who lives here is a man of great sophistication and that the inside is as perfect a combination of the antique and modern as the outside.

Find a door in the back wing facing the gateway. This opens on a passageway that leads to the Rue du Petit Pont, only a stone's throw from where the Petit Châtelet once stood at the river's edge, guarding its bridge to the Ile de la Cité. If you walk through and look to your right, you will see the Petit Pont.

Back in the courtyard, the third side is occupied by a small one-story house, **No. 16,** on the Rue St. Julien le Pauvre. Leave this quiet spot, where you often hear birds singing, go back out to the street, and look at the house from the front. We wonder what goes on inside as we peer through the glass of the stone doorway. We have never seen anyone come or go, except for a fellow who was polishing a Mercedes in the garage. He gave us no information, no matter how subtly or directly we tried. It is one beauty of a house, and we wish it were ours.

CHURCH OF ST. JULIEN LE PAUVRE

Visit the odd church of St. Julien le Pauvre. Before you is a truncated edifice with a lopsided pediment crowning a flat improvised facade, the remains of a thirteenth-century pillar, and an iron-caged well flanking the front portal. There is much to tell about St. Julien himself, and you may wish to sit inside the church (cool in summer, warm in winter) and read his story, which supposedly took place in the first century.

Julien, the son of a noble family, was an avid hunter. One day Julien was having excellent luck in the forest; he had killed a doe and its mother and was about to shoot the stag when the animal turned and spoke to him. "How darest thou kill my family and pursue me, thou who wilt one day kill thine own father and mother?" Julien was staggered by these words and swore a sacred oath that he would never hunt again. Also, to prevent the fulfillment of the prediction, he quit his parents' castle and went off to serve the king.

In the course of his duty Julien traveled to distant lands, where he fought so valiantly that the king knighted him and rewarded him with a castle and the hand in marriage of the widow of a rich lord. The couple lived together very happily, except for Julien's irrepressible passion for the hunt. One morning his wife encouraged him to go into the forest, saying that he had abstained long enough and, besides, it could in no

Church of St. Julien le Pauvre, with Notre Dame in the background

way affect his parents. Julien succumbed and set out to hunt. He had terrible luck, though, imagining game in every thicket and yet killing nothing.

In Julien's absence an old and travel-weary couple arrived at his castle. His wife took them in and, as they conversed, discovered they were Julien's parents, who had searched for him everywhere since his unexplained departure. She welcomed them heartily and invited them to stay, offering them her own bedroom.

When Julien returned from the hunt, tired and frustrated, he went straight to the bedroom to rest. Opening the door he perceived two figures in his bed and flew into a rage. "This is the reason my wife encouraged me to hunt," he said to himself, and he drew his sword and slew the sleeping figures. At that his wife came to tell him the good news of his parents' arrival. When Julien realized what he had done, he wept bitterly: "What will become of me, most unfortunate man? It is my dear parents I have killed. I have fulfilled the promise of the stag on the very day that I broke my vow never to hunt again. I will enjoy no rest until I know God has accepted my repentance."

With these words he resolved to abandon his estate and fortune in order to do penance. His wife would not let him leave alone, and so the two settled on the shores of a large river, ferrying people across the water and offering them lodgings in the small guest house that they built on this spot.

One bleak winter night, when Julien had gone to bed exhausted, there was a knock at the door. A half-frozen, half-dead stranger stood there asking first for hospitality and then to be rowed across the river. Julien brought him into his own bed and treated him with care. Later, as he was ferrying him across the river, the stranger who had been so hideous moments before was suddenly transformed into a radiant angel. He said, "Julien, the Lord sent me to tell thee that thy repentance has been accepted and that thy wife and thyself will soon be able to rest in God."

This story is pictured in a remarkable fourteenth-century stone relief, which is now fixed onto the facade of a modern movie theater around the corner at No. 42 Rue Galande, which we shall see later.

Not only was the large river where Julien and his wife settled the Seine, but the site of their house later became the junction of the two main Roman roads from Paris to the south: The Rue

St. Jacques led to Orléans, and the Rue Galande led to Lyons and Italy. Actual proof of the existence of an oratory and a hostelry on this spot dates from the sixth century, when Bishop Gregory of Tours visited the area and the church of St. Julien in particular. Records have been found stating that he gave a midnight mass here in 587.

Both the hostelry and oratory were destroyed in 866 by the Norman invaders. The church was rebuilt much later, between 1170 and 1240. Much of that structure remains today, making St. Julien the oldest church in Paris. Although Notre Dame was started a few years earlier, it was not completed until 190 years later, in 1330. Only parts of the church of St. Germain des Prés (the belltower, the bases of two towers, and part of the nave) are older, but at the time it was built, it was outside the city walls, so it doesn't count for strict antiquarians. St. Julien le Pauvre is a poor church by comparison with the other two. Thus, it has neither bell tower nor transept, but it does have lots of pillars.

What the church lacks in appearance, it makes up in colorful history. The original center of learning in Paris was Notre Dame in the Ile de la Cité, and it was Peter Abelard, the famous (and notorious) theologian-philosopher, who broke with established doctrine there at the beginning of the twelfth century and led a massive student exodus to Saint Julien le Pauvre on the Left Bank. Three thousand rebels went along with him, thereby creating what became known as the Latin Quarter, that is, the quarter of Latin-speaking clerics.

St. Julien le Pauvre became the official seat of the newly chartered University of Paris and enjoyed the privilege of holding the election of the *Rector Magnificus* and of hearing a sermon every two years restating the rights of students and teachers. The church grew rich and built a network of underground cells to house over 100 monks. In time, however, the center of instruction shifted south, and by 1449 the 50 monks had been reduced to a lonely 3.

In 1525 the church was almost destroyed. Students, unhappy over the election of a new rector, proceeded to break chairs, windows, furniture, and statues, so that the church had to be closed. With closure came neglect: An appraiser of 1640 noted that the rain and weather penetrated the building "as if it were open countryside." This is why the present entrance stands far back from the original front of the church, which stood about where the street runs now. The whole entry hall was on the point of collapse and had to be removed in the middle of the seventeenth century. All that's left are the ravaged thirteenth-century pillar with thin colonnets above, on the left side, and the twelfth-century flowering well, on the right.

Beside the well lie two huge slabs of stone that date from the fourth century but were unearthed as recently as 1926. These stones formed part of the famous Roman road that became the Rue St. Jacques.

After its long period of abandonment, the church and its land were ceded in 1655 to the Hôtel Dieu or city hospital. The hospital restored the remains of the church sufficiently to serve as a chapel. During the French Revolution, however, more than a hundred years later, the chapel, along with so many other churches, was shut down. (That was very unfortunate, because hospital care in those days was to be avoided like the plague, and prayer was said to account for much of the healing that took place.) St. Julien continued to suffer ignominy and was used alternately as a salt storehouse, as fairgrounds for wool merchants, and as a flour granary. Old photographs in the 1800s show barrels of goods piled on the *parvis*, the terrace in front of the entrance. Houses and stores leaned against the church, glad to use its wall as one of theirs.

Sometime after the Hôtel Dieu took over St. Julien and its property, it built two wide three-story annexes on the Left Bank facing the river, between the Petit Pont and the Pont au Double. These massive additions blocked off a view of the river and darkened the streets in this area. Photographs taken from in front of the church looking toward the Seine show a street that looks like a dead end. The buildings were finally taken down in 1877, when the hospital confined itself to its historic location on the Ile de la Cité next to Notre Dame. The city fathers decided then that no structure would ever again be built on this spot. That is why we are so fortunate today as to have two green pockets on the banks of the Seine on the Quai de Montebello.

It was one thing to demolish these squat sick wards; it was quite another to tear down St. Julien itself. That may seem scarcely credible, but in fact an extension of the Rue Monge (what is now the Rue Lagrange) was planned that would have cut into this area and gone right through the church to the Rue St. Jacques. At the last minute, as is so often the case when it comes to saving historical monuments, the plans were revoked, and St. Julien and the intimate neighborhood remained intact.

Now let us look at the inside of the church—with its uncomplicated interior. You may be surprised to see a rood screen (iconostasis) with three doors and six rows of icons in front of the altar. There is a simple explanation for these unexpected objects. In 1889 the unused church was given by the archdiocese of Paris to the Greek Catholic community, the Melchites. The service, sung in Greek, can be heard Sunday mornings.

Most striking is the tremendous number of twelfth-century columns, in this small area. The capitals, like those in Notre Dame, are decorated with leaf and fern patterns, except for one on the right-hand side nearest the screen. Four harpies—birdlike women with wings—peer down at you, warning perhaps of the wages of sin. Storytelling on capitals is typical of the earlier Romanesque style of architecture. Notice also the

Well and road stone in the parvis of the church of St. Julien le Pauvre

large arabesque iron music stand to your left facing the screen.

Outside again (with your back to the church entrance) look to your left at the back of a seventeenth-century building covered with fake timbering, nailed on 20 years ago to give an appearance of great age (as though 300 years were not enough). Contrast this to the genuine article, Le Châtelet, on the Rue de la Bûcherie. The blood-red door marks the entrance to the **Caveau des Oubliettes,** an underground cabaret installed in what once was a prison . *Oubliettes*, from the French word meaning "to forget," were cells where prisoners were put away for a long time—solitary holes with nothing but a grate above for food to go in and waste to go out. Turnover of occupants was rapid. The Caveau promises to show you old prison holes with fingernail messages scratched by the dying, barbaric instruments of torture, and the lake of hell rolling by, as well as to provide live and amusing entertainment.

It would seem that the proprietors have allowed themselves some poetic license in these matters: In fact, the cells of the Caveau were used not for prisoners but for monks, while the real *oubliettes* are those we spoke about on the Rue St. Julien le Pauvre. The Paris authorities are said to be quite exercised about these false claims but have never been able or willing to do anything about them. Who cares? Once you've seen one underground cell . . . Besides, the Caveau is fun, especially if your French is good enough to follow the words of the entertainers. For those who can't, there are always the gestures. The Caveau is open every night from 9-2, tel. Odéon 94-97.

SQUARE VIVIANI

Before turning into the Rue Galande come into the garden next to St. Julien. This is the Square Viviani, the loveliest park on the banks of the Seine. Eight hundred years ago it was the scene of boisterous, bustling student activity. Later it became the site of one of the annexes of the Hôtel Dieu. Twenty years ago it was the untended, untenanted backyard of St. Julien. Today it is an oasis of green and air amid the concrete, stone, and asphalt of some of the busiest streets in Paris. You'll find tired tourists and passersby, couples, mothers and children, an occasional vagrant. Ordinarily, the French do not allow anyone to walk on or play on the grass. But you can get away with it in the Square Viviani, partly because they're planning to redo the park completely, partly because everyone is more relaxed in this part of town.

Paris is filled with parks and small squares, but this one has more to offer than most. It has the great distinction of affording what may well be the finest view of Notre Dame from its benches. After peering through the trees and changing your seat several times, turn and look at pieces of Notre Dame in the park itself. Those odd fragments of broken statuary, worn down by time and weather, were once a part of the cathedral. When pieces of sculpture decorating the church decay beyond recognition, they are moved to the Square Viviani and replaced by whole new copies, made in restoration workshops in back of Notre Dame.

The oldest tree in Paris, 375 years old, stands in this park, but not without the help of stone buttresses. The acacia tree, which still blooms every spring (a miracle of tenacity), was planted in 1601 by a Mr. Robin who brought it from Guinea. Two kinds of props hold it up: the modern straight-lined, buttresslike crutch, and the older imitation trunk of ridged stone.

Not far from the acacia tree, near the apse of St. Julien, you will find a stone slab on the ground. This covers what was once a mystical well that supposedly cured the crippled and the sick. A door was cut in the church for easy access to the well. One day the church decided to give the water away free. Suddenly it cured no one. The well was covered; the door was walled over.

Cross the square to what is now the Rue Lagrange (after the great mathematician and astronomer who helped invent the metric system during the French Revolution), which starts at the quai and then bends toward the Place Maubert. The part from the quai to the bend, adjacent to the park, has swallowed what was once the Rue du Fouarre, of which only a little leg is left, connecting the Rue Lagrange and the Rue Dante. In the Middle Ages this was a narrow way, lined solid with student housing, and its animation and intellectual activity made it one of the most famous streets in Europe. Classes were held in the open air—the students sitting on the ground and not on benches—so that, as a bull of Pope Urban V in 1366 put it, "occasion for haughty pride be kept away from youth." The ground was always filthy and often damp, so the students spread straw to sit on. The old French word for straw is *feurre* or *fouarre* (compare the English word "forage"); hence the name of the street, which had originally been called the Rue des Ecoles or des Ecoliers after the students. Classes were taught by such notables as Abelard and Albertus Magnus (we'll come to his street later); and later on Dante, whose street begins where the present Rue du Fouarre ends, studied here. (There's something to be said for choosing street names that teach history, as against numbers, letters, or impersonal designations like Main Street.) Dante refers to the *vico degli strami* (literally, the road of straws) in his *Paradiso* (X, 137) and speaks of the violent discussions he shared in and listened to there.

When the Rue du Fouarre was in effect the campus of the University of Paris, the students lived in dormitories called colleges, each one representing a different "nation" and constituting collectively the College of Nations. In the thirteenth century these were Normandy, Picardy, France, and England. In time these proliferated, and every European and even some Asian countries were represented in Paris. Thousands of students and hangers-on filled this area. Vagabonds slept on the students' beds during the day and high life among the students and their clashes with the citizens gave the street a bad reputation. In 1358 Charles V was forced to chain the street at either end and keep it closed at night. Today the old road is a wide thoroughfare, and the rush of cars crossing from the Left Bank to the Ile de la Cité is continuous.

Now recross the park, where the colleges stood, and leave it by the gate you entered. Walk left, past the church, to the corner of the Rue Galande and the Rue St. Julien le Pauvre.

RUE GALANDE

This point marks the beginning of the road that led to Lyons and Rome. In 1202 the street took the name Garlande, later Galande, after the name of a family that owned a large enclosure of land here. This was the road that students and teachers took to go from the Ile, or from St. Julien, to the Rue du Fouarre, and it remained as important as that little road. In 1672 the street was widened to all of 8 meters (26 feet) and became one of the best addresses in Paris—a place where families of the nobility lived. After the Revolution, though, things went downhill, and by 1900 the guidebooks were advertising Galande as one of the seamiest streets in the city. Much restoration has taken place on this street, some of the best in the area, and we will be able to visit a good many of these magically transformed buildings.

Look to the right at **No. 79** on the corner of the Rue St. Jacques and the Rue Galande. This lovely old house, with many boxes of flowers on the balconies, carries the name of that famous scallop from Santiago de Compostella in Spain; the restaurant here offers a dish of scallops as their specialty. The cozy dining room on the second floor of this building overlooks the busy street.

Now find the two tiny houses squeezed in against already existing walls. **No. 75** is a wooden house, a rarity, above a private garage, a greater rarity. **No. 77** is a french fry place (specialty: *pommes frites*) from which you can carry off your lunch and eat in the Square Viviani.

Across the street, the **Trois Mailletz** at No. 56, a jazz club famous for its black singers, also exhibits *oubliettes* and torture instruments. Because this building is part of No. 16 Rue St. Julien le Pauvre, some of their barbarous antiquities might possibly be the real thing.

No. 56. Hélène in the beauty parlor on the corner will set hair as each lady wishes and for half of what it costs at home; her husband is well known in the *quartier* for his shaves, haircuts, and shampoos. If you speak French, ask her to tell you stories about the neighborhood.

At **No. 50** find the iron, spiderlike creature playing some strange trumpet held in its nine feet. This is a modern standard, put up perhaps to advertise a night club or cabaret that has since disappeared. The present occupant is Paris des Rêves, an excellent gift shop, with emphasis on quality, handmade leather and woven articles, plus an interesting selection of books. Visit their crypts downstairs. The sign says they were once prison cells. In this neighborhood everyone wants to have his own prison.

No. 65 bis, across the street, is a typical seventeenth-century building. Take the time to look at it closely. Houses like this can tell us quite a bit. Notice the tall windows, which get increasingly shorter as the floors go higher and higher. Push open the door, enter the hallway, and examine the marks of the seventeenth century everywhere. On the right you can see the building stones that have been uncovered by the removal of plaster, above are the original rafters on the ceiling. Look to your left now at the wood-and-plaster technique of making

walls. Walls were built of timber framing with a gravelly mixture filling the spaces between. This mixture was held together by pieces of wood and rags, just as clay bricks are held together by straw. This filler was usually covered over with white plaster, with the timbers exposed, but the heavy incidence of fire in these kerosene- or oil-lit interiors led King Henry IV to decree that every wall with exposed timbers had to be plastered over. A white clay, which was found just below ground not far from here in Paris, was quarried and used widely in the area, for example, at Notre Dame, St. Julien le Pauvre, and St. Séverin. This "plaster of Paris" has become the generic term for any white plaster. Many walls were so weighted down with their coat of plaster, however, that they buckled and even collapsed.

Find the staircase at the back of the hall. The combination of brick stair treads with wood edges allowed for replacement when the wood wore out. The pillars of the bannister are new; the post and hand rail are old.

No. 65. This building, though in need of a face lifting, still shows signs of elegance. The house was built in the sixteenth century and was occupied by the noble family of Châtillon. Notice outside the sculpted frieze dividing the second and third floors, the lower frieze with rows of rounded waves meeting in the middle, the higher one showing a series of rosettes divided by a pillar. Shutters have been attached to the first-floor windows, although these were not part of the original design. The windows, however, have been more seriously tampered with. Each pair of double oblong windows on the right side of the house were once divided by a pillar wall, which has been either sawed out or pulled off. The two-windowed, semicircular, gabled roof is crowned by a double ledge extending from the roof line. The ledge was decorated with garlands, a fitting choice for this street. This sort of gable-front house, with a roof at right angles to the street, was declared illegal in the sixteenth century because of drainage problems. From that time on the roof line had to be parallel to the street so that the rain would drain into gutters instead of falling on passersby. About 30 gable-front houses still exist in Paris, one above a laundry down the street, which we shall pass later on.

On the ground floor of this gabled house is a *boucherie chevaline* or horse butcher. Every butcher who sells horse meat must put out a sign signaling this fact; no other meat may be sold there.

The standard used is a gold horse's head—a fantastic wall hanging if you can find one in an antique store. The meat has a strong, sweetish flavor, is much less expensive, less fatty, and less tender than beef. The top half of this shop's window still has the original bars that were used for locking up. Hundreds of years ago stores did not have glass windows, and the bars were an absolute necessity. Goods were simply displayed in front during the day and taken in at night. This practice still remains; notice milk and cheese stores, with their food out on stands well past the building line. Folding doors sometimes enclose the merchandise at night. Here, however, the horse head was stolen; the butcher broke his leg; the shop is closed.

The house next door, **No. 63,** has a narrow hallway with a winding staircase at the back. Most buildings were narrow because streetfront property cost more. This one staircase opens out in two directions at the first-floor landing, serving apartments at the front and the back of the house. Almost all these long, narrow houses are built this way in order to save space and money.

Nos. 61 and **59** look like one building on the outside but hold surprises on the inside. Each of us discovered separately what No. 61 was all about, but only after we had walked down the street at least 30 times. The flowing tresses of the lovely Art Nouveau lady crowns the entrance of both buildings here. No. 59 was, as it says in the stone, built in 1910, and it and No. 57 are examples of the brick construction that Paris has used for low-cost houses. (Rich and not-so-rich Parisians insist on buildings with cut-stone facades.) Except for this woman's head, this part of the building is not exceptional. The door is usually open; if not, open it and walk in. The hall is divided in two: The left side leads to the office of a small coal and wood business and to apartments above; the right side leads you to a "find."

Down this corridor you will find an iron-grill door, which opens to an old and beautifully restored house. Martin Granel and his large family live here. Granel is an artist who has invented new techniques of working with glass and lead. Large chunks of colored glass of all shapes and sizes are assembled on enormous work surfaces and held together inside metal forms to produce spectacular landscapes. The result is intended to be hung vertically or mounted as three-dimensional colored doors and windows—Granel's twentieth-century version of the great cathedral windows of the Middle Ages. The big pieces have been commissioned by municipalities and other official bodies for installation in public buildings, but Granel makes smaller pieces for private patrons.

In striking contrast to this work is the museumlike restoration of this very old house, done exclusively by M. and Mme. Granel and their sons and daughters. The stairway and stairwell beyond the iron grill are an example of the care taken to bring the building back to its original shape. When the family bought the place, it was almost impossible to get inside. The wall to the right of the staircase bellied out so far that the pillar of the house on the first floor landing had to be reset. The brick and wood stairs were redone with old wood that came from the south of France. The bannister behind the pillar dates from the time of Louis XIII. (Doors, paneling, and rafters were also brought from the south to complete the interior of the house.) Every piece has been fitted and finished with loving care.

The courtyard to the left of the staircase is filled with curious sights, if someone will let you in. The stones on the ground come from a former printing establishment next door, and the black print and designs are clearly legible, though backwards. There is a stone fountain and lots of greenery. A once-open staircase, now enclosed behind a wide expanse of beautiful windows, looks down on the courtyard. We were fortunate enough to have the opportunity to roam the house from the top to the bottom. Each landing and corner, and there were many, was used to good advantage. Old armoire doors concealed the washer and dryer. Velvet hangings enclosed a bedroom.

In 1198 some of this land on the odd-numbered side of the Rue Galande was given to the Jews for a burial ground. It had once served as such in Gallo-Roman times, from 270-360 A.D. In the twelfth century Jews were returning from a 16-year exile imposed by King Phillip Augustus, one of many that they suffered in different countries during those years of crusading fervor and intolerance. They came back, of course, to their old neighborhoods, at the Petit Pont, and at the Rue de la Harpe, where they already had a cemetery. It is hard to imagine why so small a community would need a second burial ground unless legalities made it difficult to reopen the first. In any event, when Phillip III became king in 1270, he declared that the Jews of Paris could have only one synagogue and only one cemetery, so the one on Rue Galande was given up. Then in 1311, another King Phillip (le Bel) expelled the Jews once again, this time for

Harpies on a pillar, church of St. Julien le Pauvre

good, and closed the other cemetery as well. The absence of any traces of tombstones suggests that the Galande ground may have been used by Jews of modest means; the engraved tombstones found in 1849, however, under No. 79 Blvd. St. Germain, have been a source of complicated and passionate Hebraic studies.

The cemetery on the Rue Galande was returned to a group of churchmen who had been given the land previously by the Garlande family. They, in turn, parceled the land into long narrow strips and sold them for the construction of private dwellings. The old map in the window of the **Auberge des Deux Signes,** the restaurant at No. 46, directly across the street, shows the former cemetery location and the narrow building lots that still define the area today.

Beside being the best restaurant in the area, No. 46 is a masterpiece of discovery and restoration. Plan to have a meal here if possible. We shall tell the story of this building as we heard it from the owners, M. and Mme. Dhulster. M. Dhulster's father, who came from Auvergne, had a coal and wood business, which he combined, as was customary, with a restaurant-bar to serve the hearty needs of his workers. The zinc counter (one French word for bar is *le zinc*) that once served them is gone. In those days, even more than now, coal and wood haulers got very thirsty. There was no central heating, so each flat needed its own fuel; and there were no elevators, so haulers had to climb a lot of stairs to deliver these goods.

The Dhulsters still run a successful coal and wood business across the street in No. 61, in that small office to the left. But what interests us here is the Auberge at No. 46. Read about the interior first, and then enter the restaurant, book in hand, during the quiet periods between meals, and whoever is there will let you roam around or help you find your way. Better yet take lunch or dinner there and make a tour part of the dining experience.

The uncovering and restoration of No. 46 began when the municipality planned to realign the street and remove part of the building, which dates from the sixteenth century. Because the construction of the house was superior to that of many around it, the owners received permission to let it stand and to restore it. Among their most successful efforts was the cleaning of coat after coat of plaster from the large beige stone pillars in front. These are now separated by sections of plate glass, but earlier these spaces were filled with many smaller panes, and originally there may have been only shutters, open for trade in the daytime, closed at night.

The big surprises lay hidden in the back of the house where construction from the thirteenth century had been covered over. Not afraid of hard work, Dhulster decided in 1962 to dig out a lower level of his basement. (Like all the basements in the area this had been flooded and filled with mud in 1910, and undoubtedly by previous inundations as well.) A few steps down he began to unearth vaulted arches built 600 years ago. With the help of his son, Dhulster carried out 12,000 coal sacks' full of dirt and gravel over a period of two years, finally uncovering a large vaulted room that had served as a dormitory for 100 monks from St. Julien le Pauvre. All of this was done without official permission. When the Dhulsters finally told the proper city officials, the latter yielded to the spectacular evidence, authorized the work, and saw to it that the crumbled arches were reinforced by the most modern techniques and the use of prestressed concrete.

In 1969, as the family was redoing the bedrooms on the second and third floor in the back part of the house, a pick hit some iron and started the unveiling of an entire fifteenth-century Gothic window. Part of St. Julien le Pauvre, the Chapel of St. Blaise for masons and carpenters, once stood here. It was demolished in 1770, obviously not completely, and in 1812, a house was built over and around it. This window, a stone *pignon ogival* or pointed gable, had to be completely dismantled (each piece weighed about 500 pounds) because the floor and ceiling rafters attached to it had pulled it out of shape. The enormous yet fragile puzzle was then pieced together and returned to its original position. Look at it from the beautiful balcony alcove on the second floor as well as from directly in front of it.

Before you leave the vaulted window, look to your left on the ground. Here is a well that once stood outside this church window in a tiny alley. Not only is its border in perfect condition, there is still water in it, beautifully limpid. Dhulster has let himself down this deep well, and, as usual, made another discovery. Some of the stones move on pivots; that means there is still another buried cellar, further down.

Be sure to see the stone spiral staircase from the basement up and the beautifully finished wooden one from the ground floor to the second. Notice the modern skylight and the fantastic greenery growing from it **down** into the restaurant, above the round table laden with beautiful breads and tarts. If all this isn't enough to find in one place, reserve a table at night with a view of Notre Dame.

The service and food are the best: elegant but not pretentious, provincial but not peasanty. We recommend as hors d'oeuvre the *pounti*, which is a *tarte aux blettes*, a vegetable pie that defies identification by taste. The *blette* (or *bette*) is a form of strawberry spinach. The sweetbreads, *ris de veau*, are excellent and not easy to make at home. (On page 162 you will find recipes for omelet Brayaude, made with potatoes, and a *flambiche*, a dessert with apples.) During the meal you will be given a list of musical selections to choose from. We always enjoyed ourselves so much eating and talking and looking, we never heard our music. You may do better. Have a very good time.

No. 42. One more quick stop on the Rue Galande and we move on. On the wall find the stone sculptured rectangle of St. Julien and his wife rowing their charge across the river. It is the oldest standard in Paris. It was originally above the entrance to the church and mentioned as early as 1380. When the front portal of St. Julien le Pauvre was taken down in the seventeenth century, the sculpture found its way here. Later on, when the building was gutted to install a modern movie theater, one of a great many built in the fifth and sixth arrondissements in the early 1970s, the frieze was carefully boxed over, protected, built around, and finally uncovered.

Now continue down the Rue Galande across the Rue de Fouarre (on your left) and the Rue Dante (on your right). (These are really a single street that changes names at this point.) At No. 31, the laundry, you can see a fine example of a medieval gabled roof. The restoration of this building, like most restorations here, took place only a few years ago under the careful surveillance of the Services Culturels, which watch over all historic renovations in Paris. Mr. Simon, the owner of the laundry and an Englishman, is a would-be opera star who will not only sing for you but probably will offer you a piece of candy as well. He loves to speak English with passing tourists.

RUE DE L'HOTEL COLBERT

There is a chance to buy a piece of pastry, an excellent fruit tart, or an ice cream in the bakery at the corner of the Rues Galande and Lagrange. From this point go left across Rue Lagrange toward the Rue de l'Hôtel Colbert, where there is an impressive house at No. 11. The plaster on the corner has been neatly chipped away to show you the original stones underneath. Walk down a bit, past the first two windows, and you will come to a rounded one, probably once an entrance. If you have the good fortune to find the curtain pulled back, look in and you will see an extraordinary blending of the old and the new—a huge stone fireplace to the left, a modern sunken kitchen to the back, a spiral staircase to the right. A few steps farther, and you can enter the building (remember that you might have to press a button to be admitted and in order to leave) and look through an iron grill to an interior garden. Tall,

French windows look out onto a raised grassy section, dotted with trees.

The antique store at **No. 14** was the first building on the street to be restored and has an old staircase in the courtyard. Every time we thought about buying an *objet d'art* here, it was gone the next day. Cross the street again to the **Hôtel Colbert,** No. 7, a superb recent copy from a seventeenth-century plan found in the archives of the Ecole des Beaux Arts. We stay here when we visit; the price is very reasonable for a quiet, elegant hotel. The rooms are small but attractive. Many are brightly decorated with a cotton imprinted with designs of provincial life, called *toile de Jouy.*

Look across the street at the corner building. Above the number plate on the wall, **No. 8,** you will find an old name of the street cut into the stone, Rue des Rats, the street of rats. The lady in the antique store assures us the name was fitting, that rats abounded only 10 years ago. The name of the street was originally the Rue d'Arras. A poet rhymed it with "rats," and it wasn't long before the new name took hold and stuck—at least until 1829. Then the inhabitants of the street petitioned for something more elegant, which the city authorities took from the title of an important *hôtel* (that is, a private house), which once stood on the street. Why that house was called the Hôtel Colbert, no one knows, for Colbert never lived there. In any event, the building was demolished when the Rue Lagrange was cut through in 1887.

The wall into which this street sign has been carved is the side of the old Faculty of Medicine. Look up at the round decorated window, called a bull's eye (*oeil de boeuf),* and try to see into the room inside. This part of the building is the Amphithéatre Winslow, built in 1744. This three-story room is well worth trying to see, though you may not be able to get in. Our luck varied. You might tell them inside that you are researching medical schools or, as we did, that you are writing a book. The floor of the amphitheater is beautifully done in rosewood, oak, and teak, and the tiers of balconies look onto a huge center pillar that holds up the cupola like a mushroom stem. It is said that this room was used for medical demonstrations; now the balconies house a library collection. The entrance to the Faculty of Medicine is around the corner on the Rue de la Bûcherie; there notice the ironwork on a 1909 grill inside the courtyard on the right-hand wall.

The Faculty of Medicine was originally created by King Phillip VI in 1331. Before this, in the Middle Ages, only monks had studied medicine, necessarily limiting medical care to one sex. (Given the state of medical ignorance, the women were lucky to be neglected.) In 1131, however, an ordinance forbade men of the church to study medicine, a prohibition confirmed in 1163 by the Council of Tours and thereafter enforced by excommunication. Thus, there were no trained doctors in France until 1220, when several small schools were opened, which were later merged into this Faculty of Medicine almost a hundred years later. At first classes were held with the other schools on the Rue du Fouarre, and exams were given in the masters' houses. It was not until 1472 that the present buildings were started. They were subsequently enlarged on several occasions and flourished until the Revolution, when the Faculty of Medicine, like all the others, was abolished. In 1808 the buildings passed into private hands, and in the next century knew a wide variety of uses: as a laundry, an inn, an apartment building, and even a brothel. In 1909 the structures were finally rescued and restored and classified by the city as a historic monument. They now house the School of Administration of the city of Paris.

We found in Jacques Hillairet's dictionary a marvelous description of the kind of medicine that was taught by this school in the fourteenth and fifteenth centuries. We have translated this for you below:

. . . the prescribed remedies were, for a long time, limited to a choice of three: laxative, enemas, and bleedings. It was in this tradition that Charles Bouvard, Louis XIII's doctor, administered to the king in one year: 47 bleedings, 212 enemas, and 215 purgatives, total: 474 treatments, after which the doctor was ennobled. Richelieu submitted in the same year to 54 bleedings and 202 purgations. As to Ambroise Pare, he bled 27 times in four days a 28-year-old young man, that is, a bloodletting every 4 hours for 4 days, and in 1609 Le Moyne took 225 pounds of blood in 15 months from a young girl.

There were, however, other treatments: a treatise of medicine that appeared in 1539 affirms that the blood of a hare cures gallstones; the droppings of mice, bladder stones; the excrement of dogs, sore throats; boiled woodlouse, scrofula. It is also written that lung of fox washed in wine cures asthma; earthworms washed in white wine, jaundice; kittens, finely chopped with a goose and salt, gout; the excrement of a red-headed man, weak eyes. The wax from your ears applied to the nostrils promotes sleep; and Montaigne wrote that a man's saliva will kill a serpent. In 1540 André Fournier,

*Horse butcher on the Rue Galande. The sign in the window reads,
"Here, horse meat. Have confidence in me."*

professor at the School of Medicine, gave this recipe to make hair grow again: Boil 300 slugs, skim off the grease, add three tablespoons of olive oil and one tablespoon of honey, and anoint your skull with the mixture. One of his colleagues in this same period recommended the following remedy to get rid of fleas: Take the heads of many red herrings, tie them with a string, place this in the mattress and they will flee.

RUE DE LA BUCHERIE

As you flee up the Rue de la Bûcherie (away from the Square Viviani; the house numbers get smaller as you go), enter **No. 9** to see a picturesque courtyard and well. The much rubbed and heavily waxed door of **No. 5** leads into an entry with a brick floor and around a bend to a glass door that opens onto a well-tended garden. **Nos. 10** and **8** across the street, are much dilapidated but, given the rate of reclamation in the neighborhood, may well be changed by the time you read this. Back again across the street, **No. 3,** home of a combination pottery and weaving school for both children and adults, is worth looking into.

You are now at the intersection of the Rue de la Bûcherie and the Rue Frédéric Sauton (on the right) and the Rue du Haut Pavé (on the left, or river, side). The apartment building on the left-hand side, between the Rue de la Bûcherie and the quai, shows the kind of reclamation and restoration that is taking place throughout the area—beautiful work for a privileged few. It costs a lot of money to buy land in the heart of old Paris, relocate tenants (the French authorities are more exacting on this score than most American municipalities), then gut the buildings and redo the interiors from scratch. But then, people are prepared to pay a great deal to live across the river from Notre Dame in the heart of old Paris.

This little section is filled with galleries, paintings, antiques, and American Indian art. A handsome shop called **Rouvray** has fine old American patchwork quilts draped everywhere. You'll probably find a better selection than in the United States. At **No. 5** Rue Frédéric Sauton, two highly professional Czech puppeteers play to enthusiastic children every Thursday and Sunday. Check *This Week in Paris* for exact information. Still farther up the street is a food store, not the first one you pass, but the second, where they sell hot food, ready to eat, at very reasonable prices. If you have your own plastic plates and utensils, you are all set.

Frédéric Sauton opens into the Place Maubert, now noted for its open market every Tuesday. Once the square, like the Rue du Fouarre in the twelfth century, was famous for its outdoor classes, where the philosopher Albert the Great lectured on Aristotle.

IMPASSE MAUBERT

Across the Rue Frédéric Sauton (imagine a continuation of the Rue de la Bûcherie), you will see the entrance to the Impasse Maubert. The name is honest and yet deceptive. This is a dead end, but there is a way to walk through during business hours, a very pleasant way, as we'll soon explain.

First walk in and look at the charming private house on your right, set in the exact middle of a garden. The interior, part of which you can glimpse through the window, is spacious though small. A free staircase leads up to the bedrooms from the middle of the living room, a bubble in the dining room ceiling and a sheer glass wall let the light of the garden in. The family showed us a picture of the house at the time of purchase. They could see nothing but the side of a wall; the house was completely covered by houses against it and over it. The dead end was blocked with shacks and sheds of every sort. It took imagination and daring, lots of work and time to renovate the building. It was on this same spot that one of the first "colleges" in Paris stood: In 1206 a college of Constantinople was created for Greek students, conveniently close to Place Maubert and the Rue du Fouarre.

You have no doubt noticed the beautiful gallery in front of you. This is now the modern **Centre Albertus Magnus,** recently restored from a shambles. Look for the nice lady with red hair to show you around. From the beginning the supervision of the restoration was under the auspices of the Services Culturels who are in charge of any work done on a classified historical building. The guidelines for restoration are so demanding that the help of the service is a mixed blessing. It took no less than five years of paper work and consultations to decide on the construction of the door to the gallery—the height of the threshold, the materials used, the means of construction. It is understandable why some people prefer to do some work by themselves without notifying the authorities. Go into the gallery. This wide room is used mainly as a meeting place for conferences and receptions. Anyone, artistic or otherwise, can rent the space. Notice the interesting staircase enclosed in plaster and timber as it was in the Middle Ages. Go down the stairs on the right, holding on to the fixed chain railing, to the cellars. The iron door in front of you was recently found buried in the floor, covered with rust. It took four men to lift it into place. To the left there is a long stone watering trough used by horses in the twelfth and thirteenth centuries when this was a stable. No, the horses did not climb down the stairs (holding the rail) to drink. This is one more instance where the street was originally much lower, and the horses used a ramp. Wander through the rest of the rooms down here, including the small kitchen, before visiting the gallery proper. The gallery, which opens onto the Rue Maître Albert, usually sets up one-man shows or arranges exhibits around one theme. A marvelous exhibit that sold out in no time to the connoisseurs of Paris consisted of a collection of prints, reasonably priced paintings, and documents of the bridges of Paris.

RUE MAITRE ALBERT

Leave the gallery by the door in the exhibit room, coming out onto the Rue Maître Albert. This street, from the end of the thirteenth century to 1844, was called La Rue Perdue, the lost street. Then it was renamed in honor of the famous thirteenth-century theologian and alchemist, Albert the Great. The street lived up to its name until about 15 years ago, when the remodeling began. Even so, it is still a dark street, with a sharp bend in the middle. Walk to your right a little way to see the constrast between the dilapidated and restored buildings, although the basic structure of all the buildings is noticeably the same. We know two of the people on the street and have been able to see something from the inside: The seventeenth and twentieth centuries are fabulous together. Enter the courtyard of **No. 1,** next door to the restaurant Atelier Maître Albert to get an idea of what these houses look like before renovation. When we went, we saw dozens of names on the mailboxes, 15 families on the second floor alone. (The names have since been removed.) Seven cats perched around the courtyard stared at us suspiciously.

If you do go in, do not loiter; above all, do not try to take pictures. The residents do not take kindly to visiting anthropologists. One friend, while trying to take photos, walked into a very hostile reception. The moment one of the inhabitants saw her camera, he not only told her she'd never leave the place alive if she took a picture, but he sent his children (instructions in Arabic) to fetch some butcher knives. Our photographer, who up to this point had daringly played the innocent, decided it was time to leave. So stick your head in but don't hang around. We were told that the building has been sold to a bank, which wants to restore it like others on the street but can't get the tenants out. The tenants, meanwhile, are supposedly not really tenants, but squatters, or so the story has it. (That's why the French call them gypsies, *gitanes*.) Squatters or tenants, they obviously pay far less for their rooms than the renovated apartments can be sold for. So the bank is trying hard to get them out, and the residents are understandably suspicious of any and all outsiders.

No. 1. The restaurant Atelier Maître Albert is located in the oldest house on the street. The owner claims that the main room of the restaurant dates from 1470—the time of Joan of Arc. He also claims that Albert the Great lived here. After that the building clearly deteriorated: In Napoleon's time the room served as a stable. In the nineteenth century it sheltered *clochards*

Entrance to Nos. 59 and 61, Rue Galande

who would come here to sleep. Each man paid two or three sous to sleep standing up with his crossed arms supporting him on an outstretched rope. When his time was up, the owner would unhook the cord and let it drop. Those who needed more rest, and could pay for it, could then stay on for the next period. The others had to get out. Business was brisk, especially in bad weather, when many ropes were hung across the room.

Today, the restaurant is romantic, with swings rather than bar stools and candlelit corners for coffee after dinner. Cooking is simple but good. A large buffet table is laden with hors d'oeuvres, salads, and sausages—offering a meal in itself. But after that comes the main dish of meat, fowl, or fish grilled over a large brazier of coals. This is a good place to choose when French liver trouble or weight gain has set in. The recipe for scallops *en brochette* is on p. 163. The price is not high and service is excellent.

As you near the quai, take in the picturesque square, no special name, with its restaurant and flower boxes, its antique store, its crazy parking. On the right enter the courtyard of the corner apartment house. The architect Daladier, son of the former Prime Minister, lives here. He is the man who planned and promoted the restoration of the Rue Maître Albert. Here you'll find one more beautiful courtyard, perhaps the best.

QUAI DE MONTEBELLO

Now cross the heavily trafficked Quai de Montebello to the river, and as you turn left toward the Pont au Double you will pass in front of the famous bookstalls of Paris. The booksellers (*bouquinistes*) represent one of the oldest trades in Paris, and one that has changed the least. The men and women who are lucky enough to get a spot on the parapet to hang their metal boxes consider themselves a special breed. They love the outdoors and the freedom to open and close at will. Literally and figuratively they have no overhead. When the quai is quiet, they sit and read, or sleep, or knit, or smoke, or play chess with their neighbors. Story has it that they are never sick and live to very old age. Most of them have a specialty, but many buy whatever looks salable.

The real fear of the *bouquinistes* is the automobile. The noise is deafening, the air polluted, and the traffic so wide and steady that they see themselves under siege. And rightly so. Although plans to transform the quai have been abandoned, the fear is always there. It was President Giscard d'Estaing who stepped in to protect traditional Paris. He forced the Paris Council to abandon its planned motorway by withdrawing the state's 40 percent financial contribution.

We found the stalls between the Petit Pont and the Pont au Double more interesting than those toward the Pont St. Michel. On the corner of the Pont de Notre Dame, at stall **No. 102,** M. Lelue sells old and beautiful leatherbound books, mostly of the eighteenth century. He has a private collection of more than 50,000 volumes. If you are especially interested, he might invite you to his home to do some serious buying. Lelue also restores old manuscripts. One day he showed us a medieval Arab manuscript bound in crumbling leather and clasped in bronze fittings that he hoped to revive in about a month. We must warn you that he is not always pleasant; he says so himself. His books mean too much to him, and he is exasperated by the careless handling—as well as the occasional "rip-off"—they get from passersby. Life can be very disagreeable if one has to be always on the watch, especially here at the bookstalls on the banks of the Seine.

Opposite Shakespeare and Co. on the Quai de Montebello, is the stall of M. Korb, a postcard dealer who is president of the Bouquiniste Union. He took on the task because he felt these independent individualists would have more *esprit de corps* than normal businessmen. He has since learned that they hate to pay even six dollars a year in dues, and he often spends his own money on stationery and postage. Korb's postcards are fascinating. Often the messages on the back are as wonderful as the photography and style of the card itself.

Two stalls down toward the Petit Pont M. Lanoizelée has a serious stand. He collects first editions, many of which have inscriptions from the author on the flyleaf. The young man who runs this stall has a flair and assurance about him that the old-timers don't have. He has probably never seen hard times. There is an optimistic breed of young men and women in the antique business today who are bringing a new and fresh outlook to an old trade.

The rest of the bookstalls offer the usual fare of pages torn from old books, reproductions of Daumier prints, and modern paintings of children with very large liquid eyes. It is worth browsing. From our apartment window we even saw one dealer pull out some "feelthy pictures" to sell to an habitué who drew up in an automobile. Contrary to legend, the French are more puritanical about these things than we are (in spite of our Puritan fathers). Sex shops hardly exist in Paris, because of stricter controls on pornography than elsewhere in Europe.

If you are ready for more Pariswalks, the Blvd. St. Michel is the starting point of Walk 2. If you haven't had three lunches and four snacks along the way, stop for one, and then go on to the Rue de la Huchette. Or you might, at this point, visit one or more of the spectacular monuments in the area, such as Notre Dame, La Sainte Chapelle, the Sorbonne, the Cluny Museum, or a dozen other places that are within easy walking distance.

La Huchette

METRO: St. Michel

BUS: No. 21, 24, 27, 38, 47, 58, 63, 70, 81, 86 (within three blocks of Place St. Michel)

STREETS: Rue de la Huchette, Rue Xavier Privas, Rue du Chat qui Pêche, Rue St. Jacques, Rue St. Séverin, Rue de la Harpe, Rue de la Parcheminerie, Rue Boutebrie.

> *Voici la Rue de la Huchette*
> *Mais prends bien garde à ta pochette.*
>
> This is the Rue de la Huchette.
> But better watch out for your wallet.

RUE DE LA HUCHETTE

When you leave the Blvd. St. Michel and turn left into the Rue de la Huchette to the point where the street narrows, imagine yourself back in the Middle Ages. This neighborhood of tangled streets and narrow houses looks in many ways the same as it did hundreds of years ago. Except that the land then sloped down to the water's edge instead of rising to the level of the present dikes of the Seine, this quarter is the same maze it was in the twelfth century, although the houses date from the seventeenth.

Baron Georges Haussmann, Napoleon III's famous city planner, cut wide swathes of boulevards (St. Jacques, St. Michel, St. Germain) all around this neighborhood but barely touched the interior. He did, however, widen the western entrance to Huchette, which is why the houses from St. Michel to the Hôtel Mt. Blanc are only—only, mind you—nineteenth century.

Just before you enter the old Rue de la Huchette you will see, to the left, the **Hôtel Mt. Blanc,** an attractive, white, windowpaned inn, a peaceful spot on a very lively street. The sitting room of the hotel is decorated with fascinating sketches of this area, including one of the great fire on the Petit Pont. (See Walk 1 for a longer discussion of this.) If you do happen to choose to stay here, always take a room on the courtyard away from the noise—good advice anywhere. Beware of some rooms that are too small. It was in one of the back rooms of this hotel that Elliot Paul started writing his nostalgic, intimate account of the life of the Rue de la Huchette, *The Last Time I Saw Paris.* (The title is taken from the song of the same name, which recalled the happiness and sweetness of Paris before the German occupation.)

Outside the hotel, against the wall that juts out and narrows the street, you will see a World War II resistance plaque. Before the Allies entered Paris, street fighting broke out all over this area. There were barricades at each end of Huchette. Just across the Seine, Parisians liberated the Prefecture of Police from Nazi control and used it as a vantage point for shots at the enemy. One of the tragedies of fighting on the Rue de la Huchette is recorded on this tablet. "Here fell Jean Albert Vouillard, dead in the course of duty, killed by the Gestapo the 17th of May, 1944, at 20 hours. Rainbow." Rainbow is the name of his cell of resistance fighters. Do not look for bullet holes in the wall; it has been replastered and wiped clean.

Across the street at **No. 23** you will find the smallest theater in Paris. It plays Ionesco—*The Bald Soprano* and *The Lesson*—the same plays for 18 years. The theater holds 79, seated straight across the room, no aisle. If you visit after three in the afternoon, try the door to the box office, then smile nicely at the lady who sells the tickets, open the inside door, accustom your eyes to the dark, and get a glimpse of this tiny, funny theater. If you attend a performance at night, the intermission is almost as good as the play; this street is really a night street. Push across the street to the Tunisian bakery for one of their delicious, giant beignets, before going back to see the rest of the play.

In the fourteenth and fifteenth centuries Huchette was called the Rue de Rôtisseurs, the street of roasters. Whole sheep and oxen turned on spits over open wood fires, and beggars held up their bread to soak up the smoke and smell. A Papal delegate called it "verily stupendous." Today Greek and Arab restaurants have returned the street to its old activity, and the roasting goes on. Starting at 2 p.m. the lambs and pigs turn and crackle on the spits. The sight takes getting used to. The stacks of kebabs, ready for the grill, wait for your order. But prices are

Tunisian bakery, Rue de la Huchette

higher than you would expect; the a la carte menu mounts
speedily. Read the posted menu carefully before entering any
of the restaurants; we spent $10 a person for lunch one day
because we walked blithely in, confident that all would be
reasonable. The food is good. Some couscous restaurants here—
the smaller the better—will serve you dinner very cheaply.

Today 29 of the 33 addresses on the street have been turned
into restaurants, bakeries, cabarets, and jazz clubs. The noise
and crowds make living there difficult, but if you like excitement
and spectacle you couldn't pick a better spot.

The **Tunisian pastry shops** give the street its decorative and
fairlike air. The large North African population in this area
consists mostly of immigrants from Tunisia. They operate very
successful restaurants, bakeries, and small hotels. The rich
crusts of honey and pastel cakes are as sweet and sticky as they
look. Try **one.** Visit the beignet man on the corner of Huchette
and Xavier Privas. He works in front of his open window much
the way the tailors and carpenters did in the olden days. He sells

over 300 beignets a day, but this does not stop him from complaining that no one passes by his shop. Beignets! Hot!

XAVIER PRIVAS

You are now at the crossing of Xavier Privas and Huchette. Xavier Privas was the name of a famous singer from Montmartre in the 1920s, and although that is not particularly interesting, the previous names for the street were. At first this part, from Huchette to St. Séverin (to your right) was known as Sac à Lie, bags of lee. Lees are the dregs of wine, which, when dried, were used to prepare and clean leather hides and parchment. That was in the days when streets were known by their activity. Since few people could read, written street names were not posted until 1729. With time and the disappearance of the sacks of lee, the street name slipped from Sac à Lie to Saqualie and was finally engraved into No. 19, up the street, as Zacharie in the seventeenth century, and there it has remained for almost 200 years.

The part of the street that runs from Huchette to the quai used to run down, not up, to the Seine and was filled with the life and business of fishing scows, which were moored at the bottom of the street. Because of a history of "incidents" and general filth, the street was gated in during the first half of the seventeenth century. Today Xavier Privas is as clean (or dirty) as any street in Paris. For a moment, however, it rivaled its medieval reputation. In November 1972 the Paris garbage men went on strike, and Xavier Privas received special attention. You will notice that there are no entry doors on this small section of the street between Huchette and the river. No one's territory—so everyone dumped. One morning the pile reached over six feet, and the army was forced to come down and shovel away the mountain of garbage.

As for incidents, the street has not lost its old vigor. Our bedrooms looked down on this street, and at any and all hours of the night we heard shouts and screams and songs. One night when militants were trying to mount a demonstration, the riot police plowed up this street, six abreast and eight deep, driving young and old before them like chaff in the wind.

Each morning, however, the paths (no more cars since January 1972) take on the most picturesque and old-fashioned garb. The shop- and innkeepers are outside in their white aprons washing their windows and their walks; the residents stop and talk or hurry about with their baskets of bread and meat. Huchette boasts a butcher, a baker, and there was once even a candle-maker; in fact, Xavier Privas from the Rue de la Huchette to the quai was once called the street of three candle-makers.

Find the butcher shop a few doors down from this corner; **No. 17,** Rue de la Huchette. Although you're about to buy a picture-book slice of *entrecôte,* a rib steak without the bone, you can buy a tasty slice of duck pâté and be very nicely served by M. Bohard. Mme. Bohard, as is the custom in France, keeps the cash box and chats with the customers about the new baby as well as the state of the world.

No. 14. On Rue de la Huchette stand across the street in front of the movie house and look up this wide (five windows), handsome seventeenth-century building. The ironwork of the balconies is hand wrought, made to order for the owner. He had his initials laced into the decoration, "D C," except for two windows, on the first floor, which say "Y" very clearly. There is still another "Y" to be found. You can see it on the stone space between the two windows—an iron circle with a graceful "Y" incised in its center. What is it all about? You couldn't possibly guess today, but the shoppers of 250 years ago understood its meaning. The letter "Y" (called a Greek "i" in French, *i grec,* pronounced "e-grek") advertised the wares of the shop below. Since few people were literate then, signs told their message in pictures and symbols. This shop was a *mercerie*—selling needles and sewing materials. There was also an important article of clothing sold here. It was a garter (no buttons in those days), which tied a man's knickers to his leggings. The tie was a *lie* (as in our word "liaison"), and knickers were *gregues.* One of La Fontaine's rabbits has a pair; in a moment of danger he *"tire ses gregues"* (hikes up his knickers) and runs away. When you put the tie and the knickers together (the *lies* and the *gregues*) you hear *l'i grec.* Now look once more at the incised "Y" on the wall between the windows—it looks like a garter. There are more of these amusing rebuses, called *calembours,* left in Paris, one close by on St. Séverin.

RUE DU CHAT QUI PECHE

And now look down the alley at one of the most nondescript

but most described streets in Paris—the street of the fishing cat. It took its name from a sign that hung above a store, no doubt a fish store, though no source ever states it as such. The store is, of course, no more, but a modern version of the sign (pictured on the cover of this book) hangs up the street near the corner of Huchette and the Rue du Petit Pont. Before the street took its present name, it was called the Rue des Etuves, the street of steam baths. There were a half-dozen such streets and alleys in the Paris of the late thirteenth century, and some 26 bathing establishments. Every morning the crier was out on the street calling to prospective clients: *"Li bains sont chaut, c'est sanz mentir!"* (The baths are hot—no fooling!) They were hot in more ways than one. Many of them provided mixed bathing and supplementary services; as one preacher warned his flock: "Ladies, do not go to the baths, and don't do you-know-what there." The combination of clerical disfavor and public harassment reduced the number of these establishments to two by the early seventeenth century, but there's no evidence of a reduction in you-know-what. The only result was a malodorous population. Those who could afford to doused themselves with perfume. The others . . . well, people's noses were tougher then.

This narrowest street in Paris was, contrary to expectation, wider in the sixteenth century. The 6-foot-wide alley with its gutter of water (*cum* urine) running down its middle looks and smells like a medieval street. Walk up the alley away from la Huchette; the alley suddenly widens, brightens, and then opens on to the Seine and, to the right, to a surprise view of Notre Dame. In the sixteenth century this street, like Xavier Privas, tumbled down into the Seine. It too was gated in at night, though no signs of the gate can be seen in the stone.

No. 10—Bonaparte's Lodgings. No. 12, on the corner of Huchette and Chat qui Pêche, was built at a later date than its neighbor and is the reason why Chat qui Pêche is narrower today than it once was. No. 10 next door is the "corner" house where Bonaparte lived in his poorer days in a room at the back, facing the Seine. He was reputedly dying of hunger, until Paul Barras, an important official of the Directory (1795-99), gave him a chance to show his iron; Bonaparte began his rise to glory with a whiff of grapeshot to disperse the Paris mob in front of the church of St. Roch. Jacques Hillairet in his superb *Dictionnaire Historique des Rues de Paris* summarizes Bonaparte's career in a change of address: "From this point on, fortune

Rue du Chat qui Pêche

smiled on him. When he resided once again on the banks of the Seine, it was, in 1800, at the Tuileries."

No. 11. Above Mme. Maurice's bakery (excellent *gâteau* Breton—shipped in twice a week—and butter croissants) sits a narrow house, all of one window wide and four stories high. That makes a house of four rooms, one long rectangular room for each floor, with a small room at the back. Long and narrow buildings were common in the seventeenth century because streetfront property cost so much more. Notice the absence on this street of wide doorways *(portes cochères)* that were built to allow a horse and carriage and later the automobile to enter a courtyard. Huchette was never a luxury street. The doors are narrow, and the halls lead back deep inside to reach the one staircase that serves both front and back of the house. Open any of the doors, and if a restaurant kitchen or a *crêperie* or a new staircase hasn't filled the space, you will have a long walk to the courtyard and stairs.

The **Caveau de la Huchette,** dedicated to the jazz of 1925, calls itself "the celebrated cabaret of jazz where one dances." It is open every night from 9:30 to 2:00 a.m., Saturday until 3:00 a.m. Officially, the Caveau is open only to students, but friends of ours—long past their student days—spent a night of nostalgia there dancing the Lindy Hop to tremendous applause from the young connoisseurs who frequent the club.

The building that houses the Caveau dates from the sixteenth century and was connected by secret passageways to the Petit Châtelet, then a prison at the Petit Pont. According to a publicity flysheet put out by the proprietors, the Templars, a Catholic religious order, used the cellar as a secret meeting place in the late thirteenth century. Their riches were so great King Phillip IV felt the need to suppress them in order to relieve them of their wealth. It was the curse laid by the Templars on the king and his descendants that Maurice Druon took as the theme of his series of historical novels, *Les Rois Maudit (The Accursed Kings).*

In 1772 the Freemasons met here in secret. Then, during the Revolution these cellars and subcellars served as tribunal, prison, and place of execution. The process was swift. A deep well in the lowest level is said to have washed away all traces of this summary "justice."

During World War II secret resistance cells found their natural home here, while outspoken patriots filled the cafés. Jacques Yonnet, in his strange and haunting book, *Enchantement sur Paris,* describes the street as one of the ignition points of the occupied city.

Galerie du Scorpion. Notice the little shop of assorted curiosities: jewelry, dolls, leather goods, Arab clothes, Indian clothes, anybody's clothes. The choice is ethnic and artisanal, and prices are low—in comparison with other stores.

No. 4. This is a seventeenth-century building redecorated in the eighteenth century. Typical of this kind of face-lifting was the posing of masks *(mascarons)* on the facade. Here, fortunately, someone preserved an old sign, "à la Hure d'or" (at the golden boar snout), designating a *charcuterie* perhaps, dated 1729 and placed it in one of the masks.

The club below may have an old fashioned name, the **Chat qui Pêche,** but its jazz is modern and avant garde. Big names and orchestras entertain downstairs every night but Wednesday. The fee depends on the fame of the performers. Last year's names included Archie Shepp, Gil Evans, Clifford Thornton, and the Art Ensemble of Chicago. On the street level you can eat a full meal for very little money and listen to canned jazz.

RUE DU PETIT PONT AND RUE ST. JACQUES

You now leave the narrow Rue de la Huchette and enter the Rue du Petit Pont, which becomes Rue St. Jacques. To the left, the quai, the Petit Pont, and Notre Dame; to the right, a long avenue that stretches south toward Orléans and, for the pilgrims who went on France's most popular pilgrimage of the Middle Ages, on to Santiago de Compostella in Spain. A fuller comment on St. Jacques can be found in Walk 1.

RUE ST. SEVERIN

Turn right on Rue du Petit Pont and right again into the Rue St. Séverin. Countless nineteenth-century descriptions of this street and its neighbors all sound the same theme.

"And you wonder, remembering that these streets were full of cut-throat alleys, just how any Parisian managed to reach even middle age. I never pass here without seeing some long lost villain lying in wait ready to pounce out on some unsteady wayfarer."

"All these streets, as I say, are picturesque and dirty."

"Between Cluny and the river is a network of very old, squalid, and very interesting streets."

To some degree the same comment can still be made. If you happen to walk here in early morning, when the crowd has gone home (wherever that may be) and the trash remains, you would be tempted to use the same adjectives. Bums *(clochards)*, both men and women, are asleep against walls or in doorways. Half of the food from the restaurants seems to have landed in the gutter. But at 7:30 the streetcleaners arrive, and a new day begins.

The street was widened in 1678. Looking at the massive Gothic church on the left, it is not difficult to figure out that the houses on the other side of the street were chosen for removal. The present houses date from the late seventeenth century.

No. 4. Les Ducs is a small restaurant run by a pretty little lady, Madame Duc. She is the mother of 10 children, weighs no more than 90 pounds, runs the restaurant with the help of her waiter sons and daughters, and does the cooking in a tiny kitchen in the back. The restaurant once may have been a hall or small courtyard. Her husband is an accountant, and all he sees of the restaurant are the books. It is typical of the Vietnamese women to run most of these small restaurants and food shops. You rarely see Vietnamese men in the neighborhood; they're off working elsewhere. On the other hand, you rarely see North African or Greek women; they're home cooking. The a la carte dishes here are especially interesting. Fixed menu includes main dish, rice, dessert, and wine. Try their *nem*, a filled pancake that resembles an egg roll.

Impasse Salembière. This is a closed alleyway. Once it was an open street, notorious for its piles of trash and sleeping *clochards*, who found it a haven. Now that the doors are locked at night, the alley is immaculate. They are open, however, during the day, so press the *porte* button, open the door, and take a look. Notice how the walls of the buildings almost touch each other up above, typical of many medieval streets.

Although there are many restaurants serving French cuisine not far away, the **Rôtisserie St. Séverin** is one of the few in this neighborhood. The Rôtisserie is a handsome spot, and the food is plain but good and reasonably priced. The fixed menu is just what it promises: hors d'oeuvre, main dish (try the chicken and rice), cheese, and wine.

No. 6. Here in a 5-foot hallway is a Vietnamese food store, Thanh Long, run entirely by the women in the family. Every inch is crammed with food, which is perched on shelves, piled on counters, yet all wisely organized and at hand. Add friends and relations who come to chat and to buy, and the hallway becomes a lively, crowded place. Try the sesame jelly candies or the macaroon pastry.

Notice a very low, narrow seventeenth-century door to **No. 12.** Push open this small, worked door to a centuries-old entry that boasts rafters in the ceiling, exposed building stones on the walls, a wrought-iron gate too heavy to budge, and an iron stair rail followed by a funny hand-carved wooden one—all this next door to an ultramodern movie house.

The Church of St. Séverin. In the sixth century, when everyone lived on the Ile de la Cité, a hermit named Séverin found a patch of dry ground in the swampland across the river and settled there. The site for a hermit was ideal, separated from society but close enough to receive visitors. (Contrary to popular belief, the main aim of a hermit was not to cut himself off from humanity, but to induce it to beat a path to his solitary door.) Séverin must have received many, for at his death his reputation as a good man was so widespread that an oratory was built in his memory and called St. Séverin. From that early date to this several churches have been built and destroyed on this site—once by fire, once by a Viking invasion—but all have been named for the hermit, St. Séverin.

The present church represents a combination of styles that stretch across the centuries from the thirteenth to the twentieth. There was never enough money to complete the building at any one time, so the work went on and on and still does. Before the nineteenth century architects and builders felt no compulsion to preserve or restore original forms. No age or style was sacred. All construction was "of the day." As a result the church has a parade of arches that tells the story of Gothic architecture from its primitive beginnings to its last flamboyant manifestations.

After you have looked at the massive exterior, which needs a cleaning desperately, enter the church, take a seat in one of the back rows, and take in the whole of the structure. Then look up the right-hand aisle. The three pillars closest to the entrance are early thirteenth-century Gothic and are among the few remains of the previous church, which was destroyed by fire. The two arches between them, though broken (or pointed), are almost round as in the earlier Romanesque style. The pillars are short, cut by capitals half way up their length. On the wall above the arches and above the columned windows is a simple cloverleaf pattern, sculptured in stone. Look now at the next four pillars, done two centuries later. They are tall and straight, and the arches meet at a tighter angle. The goal of Gothic architecture was to reach higher and higher into open space. Notice the arcs that radiate outward from the stone cloverleafs on the wall above these arches. The small semicircles turn on themselves to make new ones, and the effect is that of a flame, from which we get the term "flamboyant." All of this is still controlled, however, in contrast to the late flamboyant pillars behind the altar.

But look first at the pillars and arches surrounding the altar. Study the stonework carefully, and you will notice that the basic structure of the arches is the same as that of the fifteenth-century ones just described. Why, then, do they look so different? It's a seventeenth-century story: The famous and capricious cousin of Louis XIV, known as the Grande Mademoiselle, got into a dispute with the cure of her neighborhood church, St. Sulpice, and decided to change parishes. To show her pleasure with the one and annoyance with the other, she bestowed her gifts and her idea of fashion on the church of St. Séverin. The priest dared not or at least did not refuse. In the spirit of the Renaissance, the Grande Mademoiselle wrapped the pillars in red marble and rounded off the archways with the same red marble. There is more of the same stone in the shape of an altar now in a side chapel on the left. Formerly it was placed right in the center to match its surroundings. The lady was busy elsewhere as well. If you look at the bottom of the early flamboyant pillars of the fifteenth century (nos. 4-7, counting from the entrance), you can see the remains of fluting, which were added to the simple pillars. They are now being restored to their original shape, and by the time you visit, there may be no trace of these alterations. Almost every time we visited, we found further work in progress.

Now let us go to the flamboyant pillars behind the altar. Try—very hard—to find the sexton and ask him to turn on the lights of the apse. The effect is astonishing and marvelous. This spot is often called the Palm Grove; the pillars do look like trees spiraling to the top into palms overhead. The central twisted pillar is the prime example of French flamboyant Gothic. The spirals begin at the bottom and palm out above into so complex a network that it is almost impossible to trace their path. The grove has been called "a sanctuary of serenity," but we find this particular pillar anything but calm. It is known as

Dante's pillar; he is reputed to have leaned against it often. The fact that Dante roamed these streets long before the pillar was built did not stop the nineteenth-century chroniclers of old Paris from linking it to him.

Now, as you face the entrance, follow the outside aisle at the back of the apse around to the left (back toward the entrance) until you come upon a stout pillar capped by a magnificent broad-shouldered man holding up the arch and reading out a message. Half of this pillar was built in the fourteenth century and the other half in the fifteenth. It would have been simple to complete the pillar as it was begun, but here is prime proof that emulation of the past or any idea of unity of style was totally absent from the thinking at this time. And so it stands— fourteenth and fifteenth centuries both embodied in one pillar.

Continue up this side aisle toward the entrance and on the wall to your left you will find one of the best collections of votive tablets in Paris. This was the parish church for the Latin Quarter, and grateful students covered the walls with plaques giving thanks to God for success in exams. If you have trouble finding these plaques, they may have been removed. The sexton told us "they" planned to remove them because gratitude was "no longer à la mode." What a shame!

Cross over to the other side aisle (on the left side walking away from the entrance), and in the first chapel you will find a red, porphyry marble altar. Professor Raoul Gaduyer, a venerable theologian and sociologist who knows every stone in this church, spent hours explaining and telling us stories. At the red altar, however, he hesitated, smiled, then hesitated again. We waited patiently for the smile to reappear and the story to begin. This large porphyry altar was one of the gifts of the Grande Mademoiselle, Louis's cousin. But the antiheroine of this story was Louis's mistress, Mademoiselle de Montespan. During her long liaison she was concerned about the king's attentions to other, younger women. In her anxiety and despair she finally contrived to get the priest (Heaven help him!) of St. Séverin to say a black mass on the red altar to ensure Louis's fidelity. The tender hearts of two unfortunate turtle doves served as the unholy instruments of her black magic. Bad enough—but her magical exploits continued. (Here we are only discussing her black masses, not her poisoning of some of Louis's other mistresses.) Another mass was said elsewhere in Paris always with the same thought in mind—Louis and his love.

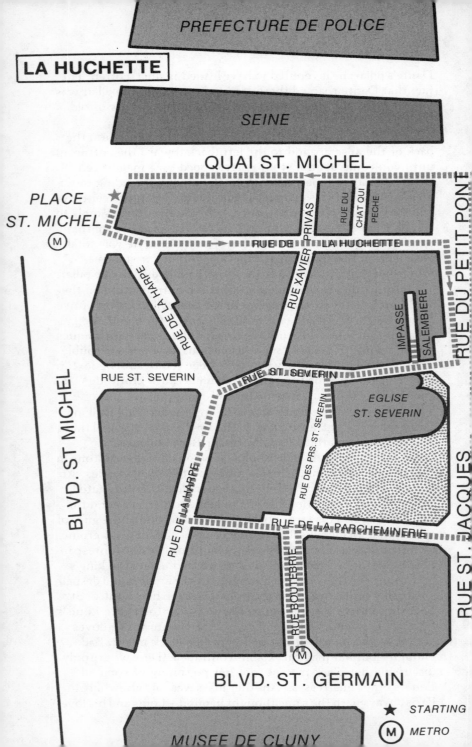

That time the red altar was supplanted by a smaller and softer one—the naked body of Mademoiselle de Montespan. But the chalice would not stand upright, either because of her curves or her trembling. At any rate, the solution was to place it securely between her thighs. All of this, as you can imagine, was done in great secrecy. Private records were kept, however, and these have recently turned up in the archives of the Prefecture of Police.

Continue down this side aisle to the chapel where the modern windows begin. The sixteenth-century painting on the wall to the right of the windows was uncovered in 1968, when the modern stained glass windows were installed. The painting is a Last Judgment. The words on the right call up all saintly souls, men and women, to Heaven. On the left and sinister side, however, are those damned to eternal Hell—all of them women, beaten on their way by devils, all of them men. An interesting testimony to the artist-priest's view of the roles of the two sexes.

Now let us look at these nonrepresentational stained glass windows. During World War II the fifteenth-century windows were shattered, and temporary ones took their place until 1966, when enough money was finally raised, and the commission was given to the French painter Jean Bazaine, a fine colorist in abstract art. He has also done the mosaic at the UNESCO building in Paris. Bazaine drew his inspiration from the Old Testament, using quotes about fire, earth, and water. The bold primary colors of the windows set in solid shapes, one next to the other, create a striking contrast to the quiet strength of the stone.

When you leave the church, glance at the notices on the wall: classes in the French alphabet for North Africans, information on the history of the church, announcements of concerts (excellent and always full) to be held in the church, marriage banns, retreat dates, etc. This is a marrying church. Come any Saturday morning and you can be sure to see a wedding.

RUE ST. SEVERIN

No. 22 is the narrowest house in Paris; it is eight feet (two windows) wide. A restaurant kitchen fills the entry, but there is just enough room for a staircase on the left. This was the house of the abbé Prévost, an eighteenth-century minister who wrote voluminously, though only one manuscript remains,

Manon Lescaut. We are convinced the inspiration for his book must surely have come from his proximity to St. Séverin and a shocking practice the church then indulged in. Each year an award was given to the five most virtuous maidens in the parish. It was not enough, however, to praise the good. To warn against the other side of the coin, the church placed the most scandalous and unvirtuous women of the parish in cages and displayed them outdoors to the scorn and tender mercies of the passersby. It was the Last Judgment—the blessed and the damned—translated from art to life.

In 1763 the abbé Prévost, then living in a suburb in Paris, succumbed to a stroke of apoplexy. An autopsy seemed in order, but when the good doctor put his scalpel to the corpse, it rose up and called out. The abbé was not dead after all! A few minutes later, the abbé obligingly passed away, not of apoplexy, but of the doctor's deep cut.

Corner house, **No. 24,** is a lovely rounded building, and on the corner above the blue street sign you can still see the street name cut into the stone, as in olden times. It says on one line "Rue" and on the next line "Severin." The "St." was scraped out here as elsewhere during the Revolution, when the passionately anticlerical populace ravaged religious reminders throughout the country.

Above the door at **No. 13** there is a fourteenth-century *enseigne,* a standard, for what was once an inn depicting a swan whose neck is wrapped around a cross. This is another rebus, like the "Y" on the Rue de la Huchette. A swan in French is a *cygne,* a homonym for *signe,* meaning "sign." Combining the *cygne* with the cross makes the sign of the cross.

No. 34 is the elegant building of these few streets. It was a stylish private home in the seventeenth century; one sure sign is the presence of a large coach entrance for the carriages of the proprietor. (The other residents of the quarter obviously were not expected to own their own coaches or, if they had one, to keep it elsewhere.) The Minister of Cultural Affairs has classified as monuments the entrance doors, the courtyard, and the iron stair rail. The wide and graceful courtyard is decorated with eighteenth-century masks just above the first floor. One is missing, however, as a result of fire.

One of Paris's fine artisans has her **Atelier des Deux Tisserins** at the back of the courtyard. A young woman, Marie Claude Lebois, makes woodcuts and prints by hand on carefully chosen and woven cloth. She would be delighted to show you the workshop in back, if the store is not too busy. The selection is amusing; it ranges from children's decorated T-shirts and pillows and quilts, to placemats and runners—all machine washable. A young tapestry weaver, Anne Laguillumier, works downstairs in a beige-colored stone cellar. Her work is modern and imaginative and compares well with the big names at La Demeure on the Place St. Sulpice. A beige multicolored, multitextured wall hanging was particularly striking. The return to craftsmanship is great everywhere but has special vitality in France. There are guides that will tell you where all the artisans' studios are located throughout the country. It might be fun to add a tour of these workshops to the conventional round of restaurants and monuments.

RUE DE LA HARPE

The Rue de la Harpe was one of the great streets of Paris from Roman days until the middle of the last century. It ran

On the Rue St. Séverin

parallel to the Rue St. Jacques and wound its serpentine way from the river down toward the south of France. This long street, which was the principal north-south thoroughfare of its day, was amputated by two-thirds when Haussmann laid out a wide, straight north-south route across the Left Bank, the Blvd. St. Michel, which took over much of the old right-of-way.

From the earliest times at least 14 different names for the Rue de la Harpe have been recorded, several of them used concurrently. To some the street was known by a standard, or an inn, or a school, to others by the people who lived there. It was the street of Reginald the Guitarist or Reginald the Harper, the street of old Jewry, the street of the old buckler, street of new St. Michael, and so on.

A standard of King David playing a harp finally won out and gave the street its present name. The standard is said to have identified the house of Reginald the Harper but may bear some relation to the fact that in the eleventh and twelfth centuries there were Jewish schools on the Rue de la Harpe, between Huchette and St. Séverin.

The first recorded synagogue in Paris, tenth-century, stood on the corner of the Rue de la Harpe and Rue Monsieur le Prince, approximately four blocks south. Nothing at all is known about it, except that it stood at the wall of King Phillip Augustus, which encircled and protected Paris. Remembering Phillip Augustus's anti-Semitism, a safe guess would place it outside the walls, but, on second thought, a more careful eye could be kept on the synagogue if it were inside the walls. In any event, the king expelled the Jews from Paris in 1182, confiscated the synagogue, and gave their houses to 24 drapers and 18 furriers. Jews were not allowed to return to Paris until 16 years later.

The Rue de la Harpe had been the heart of the Latin Quarter for centuries. Roger de Beauvoir in *Paris Chez Soi*, published in 1855, describes it as it was in early sixteenth century when Latin, though losing ground to French, was still spoken:

> There was a time when a mass of strange costumes could be seen milling around the greasy dirty street. There was first of all the *mire*, the first doctor of early times, who sold his drugs and unguents in the street, escorted by a child with a monkey which was bled by the "practitioner" **on request** [what for, we can't imagine]; then the hanging sleeves and furs of a professor as grave as Erasmus; the

flowing cloaks of the students mixed in with the jackets of the men at arms, the pointed hats of the Jews, and later on the wig of Dr. Diafoirus. . . . How many little working girls, the girl-friends of the students, did these black, filthy houses not shelter? Girls singing like canaries in their cages, the frightful cages of the seventh floor of the Rue de la Harpe. The whole ant hill of the schools . . . begins every morning to move its 1000 legs from the bottom of the Rue de la Harpe—the medical student who goes off, nose to the wind, hand in pocket, looking at his colored anatomical plates, the High School student buying a cake, the law student ogling a shop girl, the tutor taking the rich man's son to his exam for the baccalaureate. The point is that rents were reasonable; even so, no chance that a Chinese, a Turk, an Arab, or even an Englishman would lodge there. It is a special people that enlivens this quarter; a people with ink on its fingers and in its lips, an undisciplined, haughty, noisy people, the people of the schools, the drinking joints, the furnished rooms, the Rue de la Harpe with its thousand side streets is the "heart of the student."

Today it is more the heart of the tourist, though the French are still present in large numbers. As you have already noticed, the Arabs and the Vietnamese, if not the Chinese, and the Greeks, if not the Turks, have found their way to this quarter and have changed the business of the street from student housing and small food shops and workshops to one of restaurants, cafés, movie houses, boutiques, jazz clubs, and hotels. The street must be seen at night, and Saturday night is the best night of all.

People in highly colored costumes, very strange and unpredictable, swarm on all sides. They do not tell us the business of the wearer—doctor, soldier, student, girlfriend—for most of the milling passersby simply look like travelers on the tourist beat playing games with one another. Overheard or "eavesdropped" conversations tell us, however, that many of these exotic birds are settled and serious and probably change their plumage during working hours.

That filthy cage on the seventh floor is now a "restored" studio (that is, one room and a cubby of a kitchen and bath) renting for more than $150 a month, and is snapped up before the second nail on the sign announces the place for rent. This sort of behavior is not as mad as it seems. Some of these buildings are a good cut above renovated tenements. Look up at **Nos. 35** and **45** and you will see some elegant seventeenth-century houses with impressive doorways, rounded stone windowframes, and sculptured facades. The old coach entrances are now filled in, the courtyards are occupied by restaurants; but up above the ceilings are 12 feet high, and the rooms are large and bright. The cellars, once filled with mud from Seine floods or used as wine cellars, are fast giving way to restaurants and movie houses. There's gold in them thar cellars.

In pleasant-enough weather musicians and singers vie for the corner of Rue de la Harpe and Rue de la Huchette. Enormous crowds gather and often richly fill the empty hat in appreciation for good music or just the pleasure of the spectacle. We once heard a violinist who was really first class, perhaps a fugitive from a symphony orchestra fleeing the low pay scales.

RUE DE LA PARCHEMINERIE

In the Middle Ages the Rue de la Parcheminerie was the "bookstore" of the Rue de la Harpe. Before 1530 it was called the street of writers (Rue des Escrivains), then renamed for the parchment the writers wrote upon. The first parchment paper was thick and rough and lent itself poorly to handwriting. It was only in 1380 that the experts developed a grain so tight they were able to write the whole Bible in one small volume. The scribes who worked here were privileged souls, exempt from taxes and held in high esteem, though their morals were infamous. It is a little hard to reconcile the beautiful illuminated parchments that once brightened these rooms with the present appearance of a dark, narrow alley, filled with one long rooming house.

The odd luxury of the street is **No. 29,** the Normandy Hotel. It was built for a gentleman named Claude Dubuisson in 1750. One of its beautiful doors was removed when the building served as a wine depot. Each of the tall curved graceful windows, three flights of them, opened on to one large room. Today these rooms have been cut into cubbyholes to house resident students, mostly American. Mlle. Pape, who ran the hotel and was responsible for these changes, but also for the glowing restoration of the stone facade, told us how she was able to squeeze the badly needed bathrooms into the thickness of the walls. How ingenious! How expensive! How sad! For soon all this modern plumbing will be either bricked up *à la Poe* or ripped out. A "gentleman" bought No. 29 for himself, and even with the best of will he cannot use that many basins and bowls.

Notice how the street suddenly widens for a few feet (like the "boa constrictor who swallowed the elephant"), something you must have noticed elsewhere in the neighborhood—Rue Xavier Privas near Rue St. Séverin, for one. It was Haussmann's plan to widen many of the streets in Paris by requiring all new construction to be set back nine feet from the old frontage line. This plan progressed slowly, as you may well imagine. The French built in stone, and stone lasts forever. (Still, wherever you go in central Paris, you'll see these indentations, the haven of desperate parkers in a city that has long since run out of parking space.)

Much later, in 1935, plans were again drawn up that called for a complete modernization of the area, a transformation of these winding, narrow streets into neat, airy, thoroughfares flanked by modern apartment buildings. But then the campaign to save old Paris took over; the Ministry of Cultural Affairs classified every possible treasure and decreed most of the buildings indestructible, though not untouchable. Alterations were usually permitted in the interior, hence the opportunity for profitable conversion to new commercial uses and to luxury apartments. And so, the restoration goes on at a galloping pace but always well behind the rise in cost.

RUE BOUTEBRIE

Boutebrie's medieval name connects it to the Rue de la Parcheminerie. It was the street of illuminators (Rue des Enlumineurs), when the other was the street of writers. This was the book center of Paris, and Paris was the intellectual center of the world.

There is a sad irony in this fact, and it has to do with books on this street today. Look in at the library at **No. 3,** in the ugly nineteenth-century administrative building on your left. L'Heure Joyeuse was the first children's library in Paris, founded with a gift of American money in 1924. How fitting to have books of beauty and color on this street once again. We visited, all eager and pleased to have found it one afternoon, but left disappointed and upset. The teachers scolded; the kids cowered; no one was happy.

This was an example of the old kind of teaching that still thrives in parts of France and asks itself no questions. We know from experience, however, that good things happen in French education also. Enter L'Heure Joyeuse! A class will be there any

Tuesday, Thursday, or Friday that school is in session. This is one of the few ways a foreigner can watch a class in action—good or bad.

Go back four centuries and look across the street at **No. 6,** a house with a gabled roof. Gables went out of style in the seventeenth century, but one can never be sure that someone didn't revive the custom at a later date. The house next door, **No. 8,** has been restored. Try the front door. The first opens, the second one doesn't. Try it anyway. If you have no luck but have a few minutes, wait until someone with a key goes in or out and ask to see the wooden staircase—in English if necessary. Point, if you must. (We were fortunate; a hospitable French lady, Mme. Louis Dreyfus let us in and showed us her wonderful duplex apartment at the top of the building as well. There are surprises on these unassuming streets.)

Inside is a marvelously turned wooden railing that climbs all the way to the sixth floor. Each floor has a different motif and character, circles or vines or figures, possibly done by individual craftsmen. The steps are a decorative combination of brick and wood; the brick, though solid, wears off at the edges, and the wood is laid on as a protection. Many such staircases have not only been restored, but built anew in our day. This business of altering buildings while preserving character has led to the revival of a number of long-forgotten skills.

Blvd. St. Germain is in front of you, as is the Cluny Museum, but these are for another day and another guide. Instead, follow the continuation of Parchminerie to the Rue St. Jacques.

RUE ST. JACQUES TO THE QUAIS

Cross the Rue St. Jacques to the store side—the better to see the back of St. Séverin, which was once smothered by shops until the street was widened 100 years ago. The stores on this street change with time and style, but many of their names, the Cloister, the Pilgrim, still tell the history of past centuries. A very modern boutique, the first of its kind on this old street, with the skeptical name of **If,** sells ultramodern jewelry. Some of it is made by Claude Momiron, the owner, but most of the work comes from Biot and Valauris, cities in southern France where many artisans have chosen to live and work. The cleverly decorated shop is a mass of plastic showcases suspended from rods in the ceiling. The prices range from a pittance for plastic articles to great sums for gold, but their specialty is amber.

Angela at **Gingembre** will offer you tea and ginger whether or not you buy any of her well-chosen clothes. The store opened in late 1972 and already has a following of steady customers. The trendy but quiet decoration is a relief after the garish Blvd. St. Michel, and the clothes are fun for both girls and women—not an easy feat these days. Sizes up to 14, minor alterations free, choose anything from a slinky black gown to blue jeans waisted in colored wool.

In the magazine store a few doors down notice—they're not for sale—the old dolls and books about Bécassine, the beloved Breton children's heroine who looks simple but has a heart of gold. Notice, go in if you feel brave, the freaky café **Polly Magoo** that takes up half the sidewalk. What impressed us most were the quantities of men with screaming red hair.

L'Epi D'Or. Anita Civelli, a friendly lady with real Orphan Annie curls, sells kitchen and bathroom objects circa 1900 in what was once an old bakery called L'Epi d'Or. She has kept the sign above the store, the precious baker's shelves (great for flowers or a stereo), and the glass wall that separated the selling from the baking. Mme. Civelli sells some old things but mostly reproduces soap dishes, towel racks, and shelves in wood and metal. If you want an old sink, a brass bed, white crocheted bedspreads from 1880-1920, or a gold horse's head, the compulsory standard for all horse butchers, you might find it here.

The people at the **Parfumerie** are nice—they like Americans. Why? According to them, *"Ils ne sont pas compliqués."* (Americans are not complicated.) At any other time that kind of comment is a dubious compliment, but after a year of French complicatedness, we consider it high praise. Good selection of perfume and make-up here, and, if you're female, a superb moderately priced facial that could be the most peaceful hour you spend in Paris.

Métamorphoses is a wacky 1900-type store with a collection of a million little things (hat pins, silver boxes, souvenirs) and funny clothes (straw hats and old shoes). Peer around, because they save on electricity.

Baby Train. We can't imagine why the foreign title or why they use the word "baby" for this highly technical store. They have an enormous selection of electric train equipment and models that should prove irresistible to the hobbyist. Railway buffs should remember, however, that French current is different from American in cycles as well as voltage (most of Paris is now on 220V), also that trackage is not compatible.

One corner of the shop, Métamorphoses

QUAI ST. MICHEL

Cross the street to the corner of Place du Petit Pont and the Quai St. Michel, and walk toward the Blvd. St. Michel. The usual souvenir and poster shops fill the Quai St. Michel, but tucked in between are serious galleries and entrances to choice apartments that look onto the Seine and the excitement of the quai.

The **Boîte à Bijoux** on the corner of the Quai St. Michel and Xavier Privas looks like a souvenir shop but is actually what its name implies—a jewel box. This store is a branch of the main store on the Rue de Bac. It has a fine collection of Emaux d'Igny, enameled jewelry from Igny made by a special French process. We saw here some mirrors set in frames by Line Vautrin, a well-known Parisian artist who uses a method of her own invention for setting glass and metal in a resin compound. (She teaches her technique in 3-month sessions at 29 Quai des Grands Augustins.) The contemporary silver work is handsome but limited. We discovered that in France one needs a credential from the jewelry syndicate to purchase silver or gold to make jewelry. The regulation seems to protect the old hands and bind the new.

The liquor store next door to the Hôtel de Suède (on the corner of the quai and Rue Xavier Privas) advertises its products on its floor. Large squares of tile reproduce the bottle labels of wines and liqueurs. Tucked away at the end of this long store are wooden chairs that once served as stalls at the church of St. Séverin. About 50 years ago the church redecorated or undecorated, and sold some of its furnishings.

The souvenir shop at **No. 19** sells models of the grotesque chimeras that squat above Notre Dame. A horrible and therefore wonderful gift for a young person. They come in 6- or 12-inch sizes.

The cupboards on the walls of the **Galerie Michel** are filled with original seventeenth-, eighteenth-, and nineteenth-century prints. M. Michel, whose father ran the gallery before him, is both informative and friendly. The labels on his cases cover any subject you might think of—circus, interiors, romantic, mountains—as well as individual artists. Michel will be glad to give you a chair and a standing wooden frame to rest a folder in and leave you on your own. Prices range from numbers with no zeroes to numbers with many zeroes. Most of his business is done through mail by collectors, despite his location on this very busy street of tourists. Ask to see the back room, which is a small museum of fine etchings.

Musique—Neuf et Occasion has walls lined from top to bottom with folders of new and secondhand sheet music. The shop is always crowded with serious musicians. Classical and jazz guitars are displayed in the window.

Gibert Jeune. There are three of these—two on the quai and one around the corner of the Place St. Michel. They are offshoots of the older firm of Gibert, chief bookseller to generations of students at the Sorbonne and the Lycée Louis le Grand farther up the Boul Mich.

Gibert Jeune, like every other Paris enterprise that can get away with it (for a fee, of course), sets up displays of merchandise on the sidewalk outside to catch the fancy of the passerby. These take up a good half of the pavement and create a minor pedestrian traffic jam. Take your time walking through the crush during morning and evening rush hours. At those hours parking is not tolerated on that side of the quai, and cars tear along in the left lane a foot or two from the sidewalk.

These sidewalk displays are usually filled with price leaders and sale books. If you buy one, take it to the salesperson outside, usually perched on a high stool and sheltered in winter by a kind of glass box. He will then give you a ticket, which you take inside to the cashier. She (invariably it's a she) will take the money and stamp the ticket. You can then go back out and collect the book. Tedious, but it keeps the help honest, and the French don't trust their help. They have more faith in their customers, however, than we do in this day of generalized shoplifting. The Galerie Michel and the music store leave merchandise out unattended, a surprise for Americans.

The first Gibert Jeune offers art books, guidebooks, books for collectors (of dolls, playing cards, trains, buttons, pipes, anything) at remainder prices. An example of their offerings is a large color-illustrated book, *Delacroix* by René Huyghe, reduced 50 percent.

The second Gibert Jeune has perhaps the largest selection of schoolbooks in Paris; they range from beginning readers in the back of the store to Keynes on economics in the front. When high school opens in the fall, lines stretch around the corner, and students wait for hours with their list of books in hand. The store closes at five, the line at three.

The third store, and the largest of the offshoots, is on the

Place St. Michel. Turn the corner and you will literally see a book and stationery store in the street. Every morning and evening the stands are carried in and out. The ground floor has all kinds of stationery and office equipment. We always have a great time buying new kinds of pads and pencils and paper clips. For the same reason a visit to any five-and-dime in Paris (Monoprix, Prisunic) is great for all ages. Since Paris prices are even more prohibitive than ours, these Woolworths of Paris may be the only place you do any shopping at all.

It is certainly time to sit down at the corner café, **Le Départ,** for espresso coffee, fresh lemonade, hot chocolate, or beer. (If you like lemonade with bubbles, ask for a *siphon,* or selzer bottle, with your *citron pressé.*) Le Départ is a choice spot for people-watchers. Look especially at the young French men and women passing by. You can pick them out from the tourists. Most are very well dressed; the girls seem always chic, neat, made up, and slim, the boys what some Americans would consider a little too delicate. By and large, their physiques are slight, and this is accentuated by well-fitted clothes. Gradually, however, American hippie fashions are moving in—though the French version somehow looks different. Their jeans are patched and the girls are braless, but the silver bracelet on a boy's wrist will suddenly make it all seem unfamiliar. Fashion is more dictatorial in France than in the United States. For us, the number of girls and guys in tiny sweaters, well-cut corduroy overalls, and platform shoes was astonishing. Another major fad we saw was copies of American college sweatshirts. Some are for nonexistent places such as California University or the College of New Mexico, although by informal calculations Dartmouth and Kent State seem to be the most popular.

You are now back where you started, but there are a few more remarks we'd like to make. The métro, with its easy map of instructions, will take you anywhere faster than the taxis on the river side of the quai. This particular métro is one of the 17 remaining in Paris that were built around 1900 by Hector Guimard, the most important architect of the period. Get to see the facade and interior of one of his prize-winning houses at No. 14 Rue La Fontaine in the sixteenth arrondissement. Sometimes the art of the period, the so-called Art Nouveau, is called Style Métro because these subway entrances typify the imaginative floral spiraling that marked the style so clearly. Note the side railings of the métro. An Art Nouveau show at the

Art Nouveau métro railings, designed by Hector Guimard,
at the Place St. Michel

Museum of Modern Art in Paris in 1960 appropriately used a
métro entrance as the passageway into the exhibit. The
appreciation of métro entrances of the 1900s soared, but the
Museum of Modern Art in New York managed to buy one
before Paris realized their future worth. The entrance in the
Place St. Michel is missing its curved arch; this has been replaced
by a straight pole typical of the Art Déco of the 1930s, which
holds up the rectangular nameplate.

If you look down the boulevard, you will see how jammed it is
with people and sidewalk vendors. The Cluny Museum is three
blocks south, away from the quai, and the Sorbonne, five.

If you wish to get to Walk 3, cross the boulevard to St. André
des Arts. You will pass by a large and impressive fountain,
which is a hangout and meeting place. St. André des Arts is a
fascinating street with interesting shops, large, elegant
doorways that boast better buildings than Huchette, and Allard,
a famous starred bistro. We spent a morning watching them

cook at Allard and were impressed with the purity of the cooking, as well as the quantities of cognac used in their dishes. Four cooks and Mme. Allard work in plain view of all who enter; they have a good time together. A reservation is a must here; average cost is not prohibitive. A moderately easy and superb veal recipe from the restaurant can be found on page 164.

Continue up this street of little shops to the arcade, the Cour de Commerce. Wander all over the arcade and off to the left until you find some private houses tucked away there.

Look first at the shops in the arcade: a decorator's shop with copyable ideas, a modest bookbindery that does elegant work. Leather, unfortunately is not cheap, and the day when you could get a fine morocco binding for a few dollars is long gone. Cloth binding is much cheaper. The shop is always busy, partly because large-sized French books come out in paper rather than cloth and have to be bound if they are to see any use.

Now go out into the little closed street beyond and turn immediately off it to the left into a fairy island of old private homes and rich, privileged tranquility. Whenever we had an errand in the area, we used to wander in there, just to see the ivy on the walls and the baby carriage near one of the entrances, to walk on old-fashioned giant cobbles, and get away from the noise and crowding and dirt right outside on the Rue St. André des Arts.

Go on back to St. André, where there is hardly enough room to walk, through the Buci *marché,* one of the busiest and liveliest markets in Paris, and out onto the Blvd. St. Germain.

St. Germain des Prés

METRO: St. Germain des Prés, Odéon

BUS: No. 48, 63, 70, 86, 87, 95

STREETS: Place St. Germain des Prés, Rue de l'Abbaye, Rue de Furstenberg, Rue Jacob, Rue Bonaparte, Blvd. St. Germain.

> *In my last letter, I told you that the guillotine is taking care of some* dozens *of rebels every day, and that about the same number are shot. Now I want to inform you that several* hundreds *are to be shot every day so that we will soon be rid of those scoundrels who seem to defy the Republic even at the moment of their execution....*
>
> —*From a loyal republican to his section*

As you take in the busy and curious scene of St. Germain des Prés, wander over to the garden on the side of the church at the corner of Rue de l'Abbaye and Place St. Germain. We suggest you begin this walk by taking a seat in the garden and reading a bit about its illustrious abbey and the bloody events of the French Revolution that took place on and around this spot.

In Roman and Merovingian times this area, known as St. Germain des Prés, consisted of open fields (*prés*) stretching west away from Paris, with a temple to the Egyptian goddess Isis on the site where the Eglise St. Germain now stands. The modern suburb of Issy les Molineaux took its name from this ancient temple.

In 542 Childebert, son of the first Christian king, Clovis, went on a crusade in Spain to punish the Visigoths, who, though Christian, were guilty of heresy. Because the inhabitants did not defend themselves in any way, Childebert easily laid siege to their key city of Saragossa. The Visigoths, despairing of their fate, paraded around the walls of the city in hair shirts, carrying sacred gold relics and the alleged tunic of St. Vincent. The men chanted psalms; the women, with hair unkempt, sobbed hysterically as if in mourning. Childebert was fascinated by this distant procession, and when he saw the relics they carried, offered to lift his siege in exchange for these treasures. He returned triumphantly to Paris with the sacred tunic and the objects of gold. There is evidence, however, that the Bishop Germain of Paris (later St. Germain), as well as the chronicler of this tale, Gregory of Tours, considered Childebert a fool to have settled for so little. His father, Clovis, they felt, would have done better.

In any event, the bishop took the opportunity to get Childebert to build a church to house the sainted relics on the location of the former temple of Isis. There in two years a magnificent basilica with marble columns and gilded rafters was built; the outside was covered with gilded copper and gold mosaic radiant in the sunshine, and it was called St. Germain le Doré, St. Germain the Golden.

Three hundred years later Norsemen, drawn by the glitter of what looked like pure gold, descended on Paris and ransacked the church five times in 40 years, in 845, 848, 861, 869, and 885. They were disappointed each time; the true gold relics that Childebert had brought back from Spain, along with the tunic of St. Vincent, lay safely somewhere in the country. In the meantime the devastated church was left a ruin for more than a century. Then, in the beginning of the eleventh century, it was rebuilt. The central bell tower dates from this reconstruction and today is the oldest church structure in Paris.

What decided the fate of this area for twelve centuries was the establishment by the king of an abbey, with rights to the land and its revenue over an enormous area stretching from the Seine all the way to what are now the suburbs of Paris. The abbey also received exclusive jurisdiction in all religious and legal matters within its territory. The fortified walls that enclosed the abbey proper formed a square between the present Blvd. St. Germain and Rues Jacob, St. Benoît, and de l'Echaudé. The size and riches of the abbey of St. Germain rivaled those of the city of Paris.

The bishop's abbey was his palace, his clerics were his court, and the peasants who lived outside the walls (bakers, butchers, prison guards) were his servitors. This copy of courtly life did not go unnoticed by the king, who kept a close watch on the rival power just outside the city walls.

The most interesting tales come to us from the thirteenth century and concern the perennial conflict of the monks with the students of the Latin Quarter nearby. The students used to come to talk and sport on the fields that stretched along the Seine north of the abbey. They made noise, trespassed on areas that the clerics would have closed to them, and troubled the peace of the local residents—as students are usually accused of doing. In return the residents of the abbey harassed the students at every opportunity. From time to time this hostility broke into violent conflict.

The worst of these confrontations took place in 1278, when the abbé Gerard built some houses along a path that the students customarily used in going from the Latin Quarter to the playing fields. The students saw this as a provocative impediment to their passage and proceeded to dismantle these structures. The abbé rang the tocsin, summoning monks, vassals, and serfs to defend the rights of the abbey. Chroniclers tell us that an armed company fell on the students with swords, pikes, and clubs, shouting, "Kill! Kill!" The students took a terrific beating. Two were killed, one blinded, several badly wounded. Prisoners were paraded bareheaded through the marketplace and thrust into the abbey's dungeons, on the site of the present Hôtel Madison (137 Blvd. St. Germain).

This was the Kent State affair of medieval Paris. However great the provocation offered by the students, the abbé was felt to have overreacted. The students appealed to the papal legate and the king, and, surprisingly, got a quick and sympathetic response. Perhaps this was because both the Church and the Crown had come to feel that the abbey was too rich, powerful, and arrogant for anyone's good. The leader of the abbey forces was exiled; the chapter was compelled to build and endow two new churches in memory of the slain students; the parents of the victims were granted substantial indemnities. And the students were confirmed in their legal use of their sporting meadow, the Pré aux Clercs, so called because the term *clerc* denoted all men of instruction, whether or not they were members of the clergy. The students were overjoyed at this victory, and in the following years continued to exercise whatever rights of destruction they felt appropriate.

Three centuries later, Henry II, still plagued by student uprisings, decided to dampen their ardor and sent Parliament orders to pursue persons guilty of acts of violence. Its action culminated on October 6, 1557, with the burning at the stake of a student named Croquoison, who received the doubtful mercy of being strangled before being burned on the Pré aux Clercs.

This seems to have been the last major incident in the student-monk war, although their animosity produced incidents well into the eighteenth century.

That same year of 1557, in the spring, the people of the *quartier*, and those who came streaming from all over Paris as well, had been treated to a more dramatic execution at the stake. Two Huguenots who had been captured at a secret religious meeting two weeks earlier, and had refused under torture to abjure their faith, were brought into the square that is now Place St. Germain, in front of the church, and asked one last time to renounce their heresy in order that they might be strangled before being burned. If not, their lying venomous tongues were to be ripped from their mouths. They refused. After the executioner had done the terrible deed, to the roaring approval of the crowd, the heretics were bound and hoisted onto the stakes, which were placed high above the wood in such a manner that the lower half of the bodies had been reduced to ashes while the top half was still intact.

Less gruesome stories are told about the fairgrounds that were a central feature of the abbey's power. Every year for a month after Easter a great fair was held in the place where the *marché* St. Germain is today, although in those days it spread all the way to the Luxembourg Gardens. This was one of the great medieval fairs, drawing people from all over France as well as Spain, England, Burgundy, Flanders, and the Holy Roman Empire. Here were hundreds of stalls selling every kind of product and service available in the Middle Ages; troops of performers, dancing bears, and minstrels; the most impressive swirl of colors, smells, and noises a commoner would ever see. This fair served as the gathering point of students as well as courtesans and men of state. The rest of the year the area was far from deserted. There was always some activity, and it seems to have been the place to find whomever it was you sought in Paris. In addition to attracting courtiers, merchants, and students, the fairgrounds was frequented by a group of Italian ruffians, ironically called *braves*, because they hung out in groups of five or six. They were available, at the right price, for carrying out whatever vengeance one might seek, as the following story illustrates.

In the court of Henry III there was a nobleman whose mistress dumped him rather rudely. Having given her large sums of money in happier days, he wished to collect his

Head of Guillaume Apollinaire, by Pablo Picasso

"loans." His former lady, believing that in love, money loaned is money given, refused to comply. Had she stopped there, no one would have blamed her, but she continued her vengeance beyond finding a new lover. One night as the nobleman was returning home after a walk through the St. Germain fairgrounds, on the *champ crotté* (the dunged field of the cattle market), which was understandably solitary, a band of *braves* jumped him and held him by the nose, which the leader began to cut off with a knife. The victim's screams aborted the full operation, and the nobleman was left watching his assailants flee as his nose dangled by a thread. The nose was resewn, but, in the testimony of a contemporary, slightly off center. The story had unpleasant results for some of the actors; one does not cut off a nobleman's nose lightly. The *brave* was hanged, and the lady and her friends had to buy their way out of trouble, no doubt with the hapless victim's money.

Henry III also appreciated the promenade, where he would stroll in the company of his *mignons* (literally, cuties, the name given to his favorite young men) with their curly hair, powdered faces, and makeup. They were rapidly the butt of student jokes. Returning one day from Chartres, the king had several students imprisoned for following his suite with long pieces of curled paper, shouting out loud in the middle of the fair, "*à la fraise on connait le veau*" ("you can tell the calf by its birthmark"—a French pun that meant "You can tell the faggot by its curls").

The monastery reached the end of its 1200-year history when the French Revolutionaries moved in and took over. They replaced intermittent violence with the organized violence of the Terror. They filled the abbey's jail to overflowing with prisoners (aristocrats, clergy, and common people), and then set up tribunals to thin out the crowd. These tribunals made use of "guest houses," which stood on the corner of the Rue de l'Abbaye and Rue Bonaparte, just outside the entrance to today's garden. These houses had extra rooms called "*chambres à donner*," which meant rooms that could be given to guests of the abbey. These rooms, which once provided shelter and comfort, were turned into tribunals of condemnation—swift and deadly. The stories about the trials held there are hard to believe.

Once concerns Mlle. de Sombreuil, a carefully brought-up young lady who rarely left her house unaccompanied. This day, however, she left, alone, on a terrible mission. Her father, a

Remains of the thirteenth-century Chapel of the Virgin,
from the Abbey of St. Germain

prisoner, was scheduled for one of the famous fast trials in
which no one was found innocent. When she appeared at the
tribunal, she begged for her father's life. The guards found the
situation amusing and offered to make a deal. If she would drink
the still-steaming blood of the latest victim, they would spare
her father. She did, and her father lived—for a few days.

During September 2 and 3, 1792, these tribunals carried
out the ostensibly judicial massacre of over two hundred
victims. Each defendant was dressed in his best clothes, because
he had been told when arrested that he was being sent away.
The questioning that followed demanded simply a yes or no;
either answer proved the defendant guilty. After this mock trial,
the prisoners were led out of the tribunal into the courtyard of
the abbey and were there hacked and stabbed to death by two
rows of hired citizens—in many cases local inhabitants.

One hundred and sixty-eight men and women, including
several of Louis XVI's ministers, his father confessor, and

surely many "irrelevant" people, were executed in this fashion on September 3 alone, because Judge Maillard (nicknamed the Slugger), insisted on having them killed at once. The executioners, however, were soon to rue their zealous slaughter, when they learned that as a prize for the day's work they could claim the clothes of the victims. These were so badly cut up, they were worth little. The massacre continued with the slaughter of the king's personal Swiss guard. Late in the afternoon, another judge came onto the scene and, drinking to the nation, shouted to the executioners (whose arms still dripped from blood): "People, you slaughter your enemies, you do your duty!" On September 4 the slaughters were followed by a long auction of personal effects, while the pile of corpses lay in the garden, this garden, alongside the church.

In all, the number of citizens killed in Paris in the month of September 1792 is estimated at 1614. Many victims were burned at the door of the prison, and even at the door of the church, but the largest number was massacred in front of the tribunal, at the corner of the Rue Bonaparte and Blvd. St. Germain des Prés.

After the Revolution Paris was very different from what it had been. The church of St. Germain was reconsecrated but simply as the parish church it is today, and the abbey served, as it still does, the social needs of its parishioners. The neighborhood today is an intellectual center of Paris, in which the church of St. Germain des Prés simply happens to be found.

Now it is time to look at the garden itself. This quiet spot, in the midst of a confusion of cars and people, is a lacy and shady retreat in summer and a startlingly bare sculpture garden in winter. The first piece of sculpture you see is most unexpected; it is the strange and powerful bronze head of Guillaume Apollinaire, sculpted by his loyal friend Picasso. The bust sits on a 4-foot-high white stone pedestal; it is dated 1959, although Apollinaire died 41 years before in 1918 at the age of 38. Picasso and Apollinaire, the artist and the poet, were favorites of the arty café world and were courted by all the would-be artists and hangers-on who spent their days drinking and talking together.

One of these admirers, an employee of the Louvre Museum, wishing to show his appreciation and respect for the two, presented them each with a statuette. Picasso and Apollinaire thanked him, put the objects away, and thought no more about it. Several months later the guards at the museum, shocked out of their negligence by an important theft, realized that other objects were missing as well. It wasn't long before they found the culprit, and he led them directly to his friends, pleading that he simply gave Picasso and Apollinaire the statues as gifts. Because he was not a French citizen, Picasso was let off with a few sharp words and warnings; but the case was different for Apollinaire. The officials not only entangled him in the ever-present web of French papers and procedures, but questioned him so harshly that the poet was driven to ask why in the world they didn't accuse him of stealing the Mona Lisa. That did it. The Mona Lisa **had** just been stolen, and Guillaume Apollinaire was put in prison. The situation could almost have been ludicrous, but for very special reasons this experience became tragedy.

Apollinaire was born in Rome and of Polish parents named Vostrovitsky, but he turned from this background to a love of France that led him to change his name and his allegiance and to fight valiantly in World War I for his new country. To be accused of stealing the nation's treasures and imprisoned was too great a blow. He died soon after, a disappointed and unhappy man. It is, therefore, particularly suitable that tribute was finally paid him by placing his statue here, among medieval gargoyles and archways—the treasures of France.

These treasures are fragments from the thirteenth-century Chapel of the Virgin, which stood within the walls of the abbey, diagonally down the street at the present 6 bis Rue de l'Abbaye. The chapel, begun in 1245, took 10 years to build and was the work of Pierre de Montreuil. Montreuil was the builder of the perfect small chapel for St. Louis on the Ile de la Cité, La Sainte Chapelle.

The remains that you see on the two walls of the garden, pieced together stone by stone, make clear how delicate this masterpiece of thirteenth-century flamboyant Gothic must have been. Look closely at the gargoyle that resembles a doglike man with spaniel ears, on the 3-foot pedestal on the grass. The wide channel down his back leading into an open mouth show how gargoyles worked as drain pipes.

The chapel was partly destroyed in 1794, when the refectory and library next to it exploded and burned. It was completely dismantled in 1800, when the street was cut through. Additional remains of the chapel decorate the garden of the Cluny Museum.

If you have not been in the church yet, you may wish to go now, or you may enter later, when the walk ends back here. For specific information about St. Germain use the always dependable Michelin guide to Paris. Note the series of religious paintings by Flandrin, which pair stories from the Old and New Testament. The modern clear-glass doors keep concert music in and street noise out.

RUE DE L'ABBAYE

The corner of the Rue de l'Abbaye and the Rue Bonaparte is the site of the Revolutionary tribunal. It was here that the incredibly bloody hacking to death of 168 persons took place on September 2 and 3, 1792. This street was cut through in 1800, and shortly after was given the whitewashing name of Rue de la Paix (the street of peace), but finally took the name of its earliest history, Rue de l'Abbaye. The Place de la Concorde on the Right Bank, the site of most of the guillotine murders and crowd madness of the French Revolution has somehow managed to keep its name, despite its violent past.

No. 16. Return to the twentieth century in this chic beauty shop, Claude Maxim. Not too expensive for a simple wash and set, no appointment necessary. In typical French fashion, chic women are treated graciously, young girls rudely.

No. 16 (next door). This is the spot where the refectory of the abbey stood. It was built by Pierre de Montreuil in 1239. Five hundred years later, in 1714, a library was built above the refectory. During the Revolution the refectory served as a magazine for powder and exploded on the night of August 19, 1793. The refectory collapsed; then fire broke out and completely destroyed it and the library above. Fortunately, most of the manuscripts were saved, including the original of the *Pensées* by Pascal, written on little bits of paper.

No trace of the refectory remained until only a few years ago. The government was in the midst of putting up moderate-priced housing on this spot, when the workers uncovered a marvelous windowed wall that had been the outside wall of the refectory. Its two and a half flamboyant windows, tall and graceful and intact, had been covered by plaster and totally forgotten for almost two hundred years.

The wall is preserved on the right-hand side of the entrance hall of the apartment house. Some of the stones below are part of the old wall as well. For the best view of this lovely window, climb the stairs and look down on it.

No. 14. Editions Emile-Paul Frères is one publishing house in an area of publishers. Avoid the inhospitable concierge and walk to the back and to the right of the courtyard simply to see one of the smallest and most dilapidated houses in the area, with its garden of snowball bushes and holly, a white picket fence, and a bench. If the concierge finds you and scolds you, just smile and say you don't understand.

No. 12. This was a small rectangular cloister, thirteenth-century, plainer than the larger one across the street. The bays have been filled in and rebuilt, but the shape remains the same. If you look all around, you will see the perfect symmetry of the four sides.

No. 13. Here are the remains of the abbey's larger cloister (built in the thirteenth century, restored in the seventeenth), in which the priests would walk. Remember that the Rue de l'Abbaye did not exist at that time and these cloisters were in fields surrounding the church.

Nos. 5, 7, 9, and **11** are houses built in front of the church that we hope will some day be removed.

No. 7 is an old house with a crane for a pulley on its rounded top window.

No. 8. Press the buzzer to the right of the glass door of this *grand standing* apartment house (built in 1963), push open the door, and step into a marble-and-mirrored entry. Notice the spectacular wood sculpture shaped like a series of abstract totem poles. Walk to the staircase and look out on a carefully tended (unusual) walled garden and pool.

No. 6. L'Abbaye, a folk-singing nightclub, has been here for more than 25 years, a landmark for Americans. Americans Gordon Heath and Lee Payant sing in both French and in English. The French are habitués even though they understand the English as much as most Americans understand the French. Clapping is not permitted; you must snap your fingers as sharply as you can to show your pleasure, so that you do not disturb the residents in the apartments above. The place opens at 9:45—no entry during a song. Be prepared to be very homesick for the United States.

Nos. 1-5 (behind the brick wall). This is the palace built for the abbes in 1566, more than four hundred years ago. Its unusual style, which is always associated with King Henry IV, can be seen if you look to the left at the tall section of the building on the corner. The style is marked by a sharply slanted slate roof and open pediment and particularly by the use of both brick and stone for the facade. The few remains of this style are the houses on the Place des Vosges, built under Henry IV, and the apartment houses that form the prow of the Ile de la Cité, facing the famous statue of Henry IV. Brick is, in general, rarely used in France. When you spot some turn-of-the-century brick apartment houses here and there, you will agree that stone suits Paris better.

It is difficult to know how pleasing this old palace was, because half of it is black with the soot of centuries, and its bottom is covered by a hideous wall into which three holes have been punched; Nos. 3, 3 bis, and 3 ter. They house a gallery and a garage, in addition to the office of social services for the parishioners of St. Germain. Plans are on paper to remove the wall, clean the building, and restore the rest of the grand staircase, which served as the entrance to the abbey from the Rue de Furstenberg behind you.

Place Furstenburg at night

No. 4. What was once a lovely private house is now a dilapidated building of classrooms with the impressive title of National Foundation of Political Science.

No. 2. Au Vieux Paris, a restaurant, is in an old building with odd triangular windows on the right side of the house, which follow the line of its staircase. This Greek restaurant was started 30 years ago by M. Nico, whose son now runs it and continues to serve good wine and excellent food at a reasonable price. This simple and friendly restaurant is a meeting place for artists and writers. Try their specialty, *bric*, which is lamb in a crusty pancake. See the recipe, page   Between the restaurant and the modern gallery across the street stood a secondary entrance to the abbey.

No. 1. The Galerie Alexander Braumüller opened in June 1973. The owner, a young and sophisticated sort, clearly gave us the impression of being too pleased with his own sense of taste. A few carefully framed surrealist and abstract expressionist paintings share space with fine pieces of oriental porcelain. When the owner quoted some astronomical sum a Japanese buyer paid for two bowls, we asked in amazement, "How much?" To which he answered with disdain, "Money is always so fascinating to Americans."

All the streets branching off this intersection have interesting old houses and craft and antique shops. Retrace your steps to the Rue de Furstenberg.

RUE DE FURSTENBERG

When Egon de Furstenberg was abbé of St. Germain des Prés in the last decades of the seventeenth century, he opened a new entrance to the palace, one that led into the Rue Colombier (the street of doves), now the Rue Jacob. This entrance descended from the grand staircase of the abbey into the Rue de Furstenberg.

The square in the middle of this short street, with its four Paulownia trees (three new ones, one old one), benches, and old-fashioned light globes, is a pictureque spot. Although the trees are named after Anna Pavlovna, daughter of Czar Paul I of Russia, they are Chinese (some references say Japanese) in origin. They are admired in the spring for their perfumed mauve blossoms and large leaves. Symmetrical houses were built on either side of the street; **Nos. 6 and 8,** still standing, recognizable by their low doorways and brick-and-stone facade, were stables of the abbey.

A walk through the covered archway of No. 6, across the courtyard to the center door, takes you to the **Delacroix studio,** home of the painter for the last six years of his life, 1857-1863. The small museum shows fine drawings and small sketches of his completed masterpieces. Go through the museum to a small orange building with a pebbled garden. This was the infirmary of the abbey, where the invalids were kept, more as protection for the well than cure for the sick.

Outside once more, walking left toward the Rue Jacob, notice at the point where the street narrows, a stone sculptured torch on the pillar of **No. 4.** It is the remains of the decoration of the court of honor, a place where ceremonies took place, which this square was, before Furstenberg made it into his private domicile. The house was sold to the government in 1797 and taken down. Only this pillar, an entry, remains. Interesting stores—autographs and manuscripts at Etienne Charavay, choice seventeenth- and eighteenth-century antiques at Yveline, and contemporary materials at a store with a Russian name—lead to the Rue Jacob.

RUE JACOB

Streets in Paris are often named after famous people, important places, or interesting signs, but never do they get the name of an Old Testament patriarch like Jacob. The name was given in memory of a vow taken by Marguerite de Valois, whose colorful life has left its mark on the history of this area and is worth recalling in some detail. Marguerite, known as *"chère* Margot," was the daughter of Henry II and Catherine de Médicis, the sister of Henry III, and the wife of Henry of Navarre, later Henry IV. In addition to this noble background, she was beautiful and learned. Her memoirs are among the best written by nobility, but when the French say *"chère* Margot" with a knowing smile, they are thinking less of what she wrote than what she left out. We'll try filling in.

As one historian put it, "She knew love at eleven," and thanks to this early start was able to collect a long list of lovers in the course of her career. She had, of course, good teachers: her brother Henry III and his flamboyant *mignons,* as well as her cousin and husband Henry, who is recorded in history as having had 56 mistresses—but history can't know everything. This is, of course, the famous French court Shakespeare delighted in mimicking.

Margot was married in 1572 to her Protestant husband, second in line for the throne, Henry of Navarre, very much against her Catholic convictions and the will of the Pope. This mattered little against the determination of her brother, King Charles IX.

It took more than marriage to slow Margot down. She had her establishment; her husband, his. All went well until one day in 1583 Margot's brother Henry, now King Henry III, denounced his sister's debauchery before the entire court. The actual cause of his anger was that Margot openly parodied her brother and his court of powder puffs.

This denouncement made it harder for Henry of Navarre to put up with her scandalous behavior and finally, in 1587, under social pressure, her husband put her away in the Château d'Usson in Auvergne, where she managed to seduce her jailer. She made the best of her exile—18 years of a small court— writing memoirs and adding to her list of conquests. Nevertheless, she missed Paris and swore to raise an altar to Jacob if ever she was allowed to return. Jacob had also suffered exile, had worked and waited 14 years for Rachel, and had finally been able to go back home. He, too, had given thanks to God for his safe return by building an altar.

The happy day came in 1605. (By this time Henry of Navarre, now King Henry IV, had long since divorced Margot and married Marie de Médicis.) The king installed her in the Château of the Archbishops (an ironic touch) of Sens (now open for visits), located on the Right Bank of the Seine at the entrance to the Marais quarter.

Margot was then 52, fat, bald, but as insatiable as ever. Her weight was so great she ordered the doorways widened. Her hair was so thin she snipped the locks of her blond valets for her wigs. Jean Duché, in his *Histoire de France raconté à Juliette*, claims she wore around her ample waist amulets containing pieces of the hearts of her dead lovers.

Her lover of the moment was the 20-year-old Count of Vermond, but finding him perhaps too old Margot brought in an 18-year-old son of a carpenter from Usson. The Hôtel de Sens became a place of revelry. Vermond couldn't stand it. He lay in wait for his rival and shot him in the head right in front of Margot, who was returning from her religious devotion in a nearby church. Margot was enraged; had Vermond pursued and arrested; and when he was brought before her, cried out,

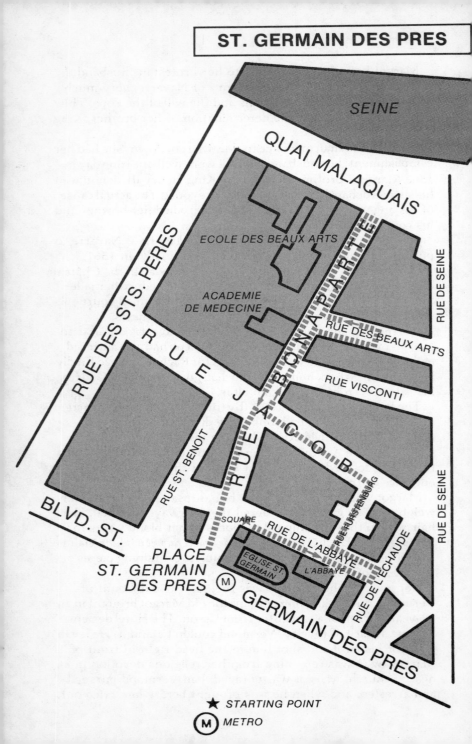

ST. GERMAIN DES PRES

SEINE

QUAI MALAQUAIS

RUE DES STS. PERES

RUE JACOB

RUE BONAPARTE

RUE DE SEINE

ECOLE DES BEAUX ARTS

ACADEMIE DE MEDECINE

RUE DES BEAUX ARTS

RUE VISCONTI

RUE ST. BENOIT

RUE DE SEINE

SQUARE

RUE DE L'ABBAYE

RUE FURSTENBURG

RUE DE L'ECHAUDE

EGLISE ST. GERMAIN

L'ABBAYE

BLVD. ST.

PLACE ST. GERMAIN DES PRES

Ⓜ

GERMAIN DES PRES

★ STARTING POINT

Ⓜ METRO

"Kill the wretch. Here, here are my garters. Strangle him!"
They cut off his head instead, while Margot looked on.

But all this blood and gore depressed her, and two days later
she decided to leave the Hôtel de Sens and inhabit a house she
was then building on the Pré aux Clercs, on what is now Nos. 2-
10 Rue de Seine. She remembered her vow and built the convent
of Petits Augustins (now No. 14 Rue Bonaparte) in the back of
the garden of her château. There she installed 14 Augustine
fathers, who spelled each other every two hours, singing
praises to Jacob with words and music written by her. Five years
later she chased them out—because they sang badly. The name
of the street is all that remains of Margot's celebrated gesture of
thanksgiving.

This street is what we call one of the hidden streets of Paris.
The unknowing eye sees store after store below 5-story
apartment buildings that show little decoration and little
difference one from the other. Not so. There are gardens,
courtyards, staircases, even ceilings to uncover on the piece of
the Rue Jacob that runs from the corner of Rue Jacob and Rue de
Furstenberg left to Rue Bonaparte. The street to the right is
just as interesting and leads to a lovely square, old houses, and
modern stores, but today we are turning left and will keep
crossing back and forth until we reach the corner of the Rue
Bonaparte.

No. 5. This building, with Scandiart on the corner (same
things you've seen at home), is the spot where one of the towers
of the surrounding walls of the abbey stood. It was 20 feet in
diameter and stood next to the dovecote (hence the old name of
the street, Rue Colombier) of the abbey.

No. 10. As is often the custom, a cabaret, L'Echelle de Jacob
(Jacob's ladder), has used the name of the street as the source of
inspiration for its own name. Despite the fine wooden bust of a
woman above the door, this is not the entry. You go through
the small door into the courtyard, through the apartment
building, and then into the cabaret. Jacques Brel started here,
where he was pleased to be able to sing—for free. The cabaret
opens at 11 p.m., is closed Sunday, tel. no. 033-53-53.

Enter the courtyard of No. 12 and go through the archway.
You'll find a small garden at the back and to your right an Indian
dress shop called **Mohanjeet,** which seems to attract a trendy
clientele.

No. 12. This old bookstore, Livres Anciens, Chez Durtal, which specializes in technical subjects, is also a meeting place of lovers of Paris. Somewhere in the window you will see a card indicating that the Huysmans Society meets here every Saturday from three to six. Joris Huysmans is the famous nineteenth-century writer who described Paris in a manner so poetic, so unbelievably full of love, that his books today are collectors' treasures and are sold at auction for very high prices. Huysmans could write about the garbage smells of Paris in a way that would make you mourn the institution of the garbage truck.

No. 7. This building dates from 1640 and was called the Hôtel St. Paul. Racine lived here with his uncle in 1656, when he was 17 years old. The gallery housed here, Antoinette, specializes in primitives. Just past the entrance you will see at **No. 9** a short window in a mezzanine. This *entresol* is the apartment of the concierge. The house has a wood staircase, which dates from the fifteenth century, the time of Louis XIII.

No. 16 is a quaint house, two windows wide, with a very small entry. Ring the bell and push open the door. The long, narrow hall leads to a quiet pebbled garden in the back. The spot is suddenly silent except for the singing of birds.

No. 18. In a new building for this street (built in 1928), the publishing house of Languereau is one of the oldest and most important children's publishing houses in Paris. Enter the building, and on the left wall of the staircase notice a poster picture of dancing children. This was the cover of the famous nineteenth-century songbook, *Chansons,* illustrated by Boutet de Montvel. If children's literature in France interests you, walk up to the second floor; they will be glad to show or sell you some of their superb books.

In the seventeenth century Nos. 9, 11, and 13, built next to the old abbey wall, were all one house, belonging to a member of Parliament, M. Chabenat de la Malmaison. Later, the building was the Hôtel de la Gabelle, the main office for the collection of the salt tax.

Now let us look at what these buildings still have to show. Enter the music store named Pan, **No. 11,** and ask—nicely, of course—the owner, a fine gentleman, if you may look at the ceiling on the second floor, where audio equipment is sold. You will see hundreds of rafters in Paris but none like these remarkably well-preserved and painted ones. The rafters date from the end of the fifteenth century; the painting, however, was done later. Various trades of the city of Paris are pictured in the medallions in the center. Pan and his pipes appear toward the back of the room, but it is purely coincidence that that is also the name of the store. The shop used to be next door, where a less beautiful part of the ceiling also can be seen. The present owner of Pan bought this building from an antique dealer, who had never uncovered what was certainly the most valuable treasure his store had ever seen. The entire ceiling had been hidden (and preserved) by plaster. Very skillful restoration has saved most of it. Imagine the beauty of this room when it was two floors high and the fireplace on the side wall was huge enough to reach this high. You will find an excellent selection of records and record players here.

The gallery next door, **Tortue,** encourages young artists and engravers. Climb up the staircase to see the other half of the ceiling.

And now you reach the entry to Nos. 11 and 13. Stand back and look at them. The tall, rounded doorways are topped by the typical eighteenth-century mask decorations called *mascarons.* These two must have been done either at different times or by different people. One of the nicest pieces of iron sculpture, resembling a flamboyant "s" stuck over with tridents, is attached to the wall above the two doorways.

Go into No. 11 (ring the bell and push open the door), turn left through the doors near the concierge sign, up a few steps, to find an imposing, wide, stone staircase. What is truly impressive is that the bannisters and railing are cut in stone by hand—a tremendous task, in comparison to the difficult one of turning a bannister in wood. The style is the same as that of a wooden staircase, and when you continue up, you will notice the switch to wood, at which point the stairs turn to stone. Look at the heavily worn and waxed wood on the landings and stairs. In summer this wide stairwell is a cool, quiet spot; in winter, when it's dark early, turn the minute light on until you've seen it all.

On the other side of No. 13 two antique stores share the premises. One specializes in Regency furniture but particularly in games: chess, backgammon, game tables, ivory counters, etc. The other is a rare stone and gem shop, some of whose petrified wood looks like slices of caramel. The lady in the shop explained that the precious stones came from thousands of miles away, from a place called, "Ah-ree-zo-na." "Ah yes!" we said. M. Boulle specializes in agate and septaria.

No. 20. Much has been said and written about No. 20, but the actual footwork turned up very little. First and most important, a little Temple of Friendship, built to replace churches during the Revolution, stands in an unused garden to the right behind an unopenable iron gate. We eventually got to the temple through No. 22, and a purchase therein, but there is now work in progress to restore the temple and give it easy access through the iron gates. The temple is low and rectangular with Doric columns. The words, "A l'Amitié" (to friendship), are inscribed on it. This neighborhood was rich in such Revolutionary clubs, but few remain. The garden and the temple are owned by Michel Debré, former right-hand man to De Gaulle and then to Pompidou. Mme. Debré gave small receptions here.

A Miss Natalie Clifford Barney, an American lady who had great influence in literary circles, lives at No. 20. We were told that she would be delighted to tell you all sorts of stories about the literary salon and show you the temple. Whether you see it or not you should have no trouble in finding the stair rail to the left of the entry. This is a classified historical monument, and it has an interesting gate extending from the wrought-iron bannister.

No. 22. Fanfreluchette is the whimsical name of this children's clothing store, where their knitted and crocheted clothes have changed knitting from grandmotherly, old-fashioned styles to those for swinging littles.

Behind this boutique, and through the entry, is the Rôtisserie de l'Abbaye, a restaurant steeped in medieval atmosphere, open for dinner and show only.

Open the glass doors in front of you, and continue through a corridor filled with odd pieces of furniture, up two steps, and turn left into the garden of M. Comoglio's antique store. You will be amazed by the array of strange heads and friezes, pieces of walls and sculpture. The store doesn't cater to a browser's eye but has lots to offer just the same. The place is dark and dust covered, but you might find a Japanese screen on an Art Nouveau table. We thought, naively, that perhaps we could "find a buy," but Comoglio knows antiques well, and prices reflect the objects' worth.

Nos. 17 and **26.** Two bookstores, which typify the extent of specialized bookstores in Paris, face each other on the Rue Jacob. One is an agricultural and horticultural bookstore; the other, specializing in maritime and overseas editions, shows maps and prints in the window as well. Look up at the old houses.

No. 19. If you want to find the best garden we saw on this street, follow these instructions. Before you start through courtyards and past the concierge, however, we must say that, in general, these highly prized gardens are poorly kept and show little imagination. Walk in No. 19, through the entrance and a large courtyard to a short hall (to the right of a tiled lean-to), up seven steps. Turn left through a gray horizontal windowed door, continue down a hallway through a vertical windowed door to the left, and into a garden. The workers in the back rooms of publishing houses you pass will not even see you.

This garden is right in back of the Place Furstenberg, and you can see the infirmary building, now the Delacroix Museum, on the other side of the wall to your far right.

The swings, sandbox, and birdhouse in the garden belong to the two families whose doors open onto this spot; they are the sole users of the garden. The apartment closest to you on the ground floor was lived in by Prud'homme, an active pamphlet-eer against the Ancien Régime. He was an editor of the "Revue de Paris," a Revolutionary journal. It was in the quiet of this garden that he wrote the incendiary articles that led to at least one arrest.

No. 23. Anaïs, across the street, is a needlepoint store that has been here for many years and shows only small signs of catching up to the modern possibilities of this art. The ladies are skilled, capable of drawing your design for you, as well as supplying their own. They send you on your way with marked canvas, needles, wool, and samples of each stitch already begun on your canvas. The store was named after their aunt, Anaïs, whose last name was surely not Nin.

In the Mood. Here is another example of a new old-fashioned store on this lovely street. Thousands of cushions, covers, and quilts fill the store. Inside, look up and you will see that they fill the balcony above as well.

No. 28. A little shop to the left of the entry is Serpent a Plumes. Like Lawrence's *Plumed Serpent*, this boutique tries to capture the romance of Mexico. This is the "in" place to buy your wedding dress. The fresh, white, narrow-waisted dresses are finely pleated and stitched into shape. Embroidery doubles the price. Attractive peasant blouses in all colors, which are worn with the inevitable blue jeans, and an interesting collection of odd gifts and pieces of clothing at lower prices are sold here also.

Nos. 25 and **29.** The three different groups of people we

Mascaron at Nos. 11 and 13, Rue Jacob

questioned as they left the Hôtel des Deux Continents and the Hôtel D'Isly down the street were all satisfied and also pleased that English was spoken. Hotels are the only comparatively inexpensive buy in Paris, despite yearly hikes in rates, which occur in March when the season rate changes.

No. 30. There are no old houses or antique staircases in the back of this courtyard, but you will find a collection of young artisans who restore paintings as well as and probably better than their predecessors hundreds of years before them. Visit Restoration-Depretz first, and they will take you to the bookbinder, L'Atelier Gauche, to the left, afterwards.

The first time we visited these young artisans they were barefoot and hirsute, seemingly anti-establishment. The following year they wore jackets and shoes, but the ambience remains the same. They move within each other's work areas, talking and joking all the while. This easy come and go, this seeming lack of concentration, is the setting for the highest degree of delicate, technical, and artistic work.

We were shown how a Poliakoff painting was being transferred from its original decaying canvas to a new one, how one and a half year's work on a Dürer was finally wiping away slash marks and deterioration. We witnessed the uncovering of mushrooms, grapes, and a butterfly that had been blackly painted out by the Victorians—no doubt as too earthy, too sexy, and too frivolous. A young painter named Lagrue had set up his easel near the entrance and amused himself and his audience by reinterpreting famous paintings, turning a crusade into a Chaucerian pilgrimage, a Renoir garden party into a Bacchanalia. We were excited and inspired by these people and wished we could do what they knew how to do.

The Atelier Gauche has snubbed the machine age, all the book bindings are made by hand, using the same sort of manual tools used in the Latin Quarter 500 years ago. Here the master, an older man, works with his young worker who has just completed a 3-year course and then spent another year perfecting his or her craft. Their books are splendid, handsome, and perfect, but no attempt is made to create new designs. We think that would be the thing to do. Professors from the United States, the shop's best customers, order bindings of goat leather, of half leather, or of woven cloth.

No. 27. Twenty years ago the Editions du Seuil, an important French publishing house, took over this lovely private home and front garden. Ingres, the champion of classical painting, lived here more than 150 years ago.

No. 32. Mme. Castaing's antique store is an odd one. Room after room, filled with strange furniture from the colonies or from England, continue far up the Rue Jacob. Elephant's feet serve as ash trays, goat's legs hold up tables, and palms and rubber plants flourish everywhere. Prices are not marked, and if Mme. Castaing is not there, the people in charge are of no help except to tell you to return in the afternoon when Madame will be there.

No. 29. Jeanne Fillon sells Art Déco and Art Nouveau furniture and art objects. You'll find first-rate signed pieces here—Lalique, Gallé, and Marjorel. Prices are high, which is not surprising for either of the two styles since they have again come into vogue.

RUE BONAPARTE

Despite too many cars in the road and too many people on the street, the Rue Bonaparte is still a favorite for visitors and Parisians. The shops, rich with the art of today and yesterday, are evident everywhere; the colorful history is less obvious but there for the seeing and imagining.

Seven hundred years ago there was no street here at all, simply open fields that belonged to the abbey. You will recall the stories of the university students battling violently with the priests of the abbey over the use of these lands. These conflicts were only settled when in 1368 the monks built a wall and moat around themselves for privacy and safekeeping. At that time they also dug a canal, 65 feet wide and 25 feet deep, which ran from the Seine down the present Rue Bonaparte to the corner where you are now standing—Rue Jacob and Rue Bonaparte.

Right here, this arm of the river, La Petite Seine, emptied its waters into the moat of the abbey. Boats sailed up and down, bringing and taking away goods. But the moat's most important function was to provide a natural division between the fields frequented by the students, a small piece of land that covers the Rues Jacob and Visconti up to the Rue Bonaparte (called the Petit Pré aux Clercs) and the larger field on the other side of the canal favored by the priests (called the Grand Pré aux Clercs).

For almost 200 years the little Seine characterized the *quartier*, and when it was eventually filled in in 1540, it gave its name to the paved road that took its place, Rue de la Petite Seine.

In 1606, when the famous Margot received a gift from her ex-husband, King Henry IV, of a piece of land on the Rue de Seine, she built the beautiful château whose walled gardens and walks cut through the Rue de la Petite Seine, closing it off from the Seine, which lies at the top of this street. But Margot was generous with her new domain and allowed her meadows and gardens and shaded walks to go on giving pleasure to the simple folk of the neighborhood.

Marie de Médicis, Margot's successor as wife to Henry IV and whose money no doubt paid for Margot's extravagance, was jealous of the latter's reputation for generosity and her popularity with the people. And so Marie tried to outdo her by building the Cours de la Reine (the queen's way), a wide and beautiful road on the right bank of the Seine, parallel to the Champs-Elysées. These two ladies, Marie and Margot, spent more time outfoxing each other than Henry spent thinking about either of them; his constant love was Gabrielle d'Estrées.

Margot's gardens and the convent of Petits Augustins that she had built further up the street lasted until 1628, 13 years after her death. At that time her property was divided among many, and the street was once again opened up, this time named for the convent, the Rue des Petits Augustins. Look across the street at the street sign above the tapestry shop on the corner to see this old name cut in stone.

The name Bonaparte was not given until the year 1852. We have often wondered why there is no Rue Napoleon in Paris. Was he too formidable a hero? Perhaps the idea of the little Bonaparte is more acceptable.

And now for the street—to find what is new and what remains of the old. We will turn right at the corner of Bonaparte and Jacob, continue up the right side to the top, and then cross to the left side and down to return to the Place St. Germain.

No. 21. Very few stores in the ample old-fashioned style of Bulloz still exist in Paris or anywhere. The moment you enter the large, uncluttered, quiet premises, and are greeted by the gentle ladies who serve you, you realize that although their type of photographic service is greatly in demand today, they remain unaffected by the passing of time. Here is where you can have a picture of yourself, or a landscape, or a document, or a painting, or anything, blown up to any size you specify. Their work is excellent as well as dependable. Pictures come in black and white or in color, and there are thousands to choose from, if you like the idea but don't have the picture.

The courtyard of No. 21 gives you an idea of the grand houses that surrounded the abbey in the sixteenth century. The garden of Queen Margot's palace on the Rue de Seine extended all the way to the other side of this street just a few yards up from here. The grand house before you now was built in 1760, around the courtyard of an earlier one, for the Prévost de St. Cyr, and lived in under the Consulate (1799-1804), by the Princess de Sohan-Rochefort who was secretly married to the Duke of Enghien. After the Revolution these houses changed their tenants and their appearance, as the neighborhood turned popular. Today high rents make it once more a street of very special shops and coveted apartments.

This large courtyard is picturesque, with its thick ivy, ornamental ironwork on the balcony windows, and large iron pulley on the dormer or mansard above to the left.

The dress shop **Vicky Tiel** is worth the visit. You enter a bright bower of plants and wicker furniture; it is a dropped living room in an area anyone else would have used to show merchandise. The dresses, however, line the walls to the left, and it is there that the buying and fitting goes on. Vicky Tiel, American, friendly, and bright, sells a few classic models, short or long, that can be made for you in five to six days. Every time the price goes up, we are sorry we didn't buy before. Elizabeth Taylor is her patron, and if you hit the right day you might see the famous lady trying on one of these softly draped dresses. Continue up the street to the corner of the Rue Visconti.

No. 19. The long narrow gallery, Les Heures Claires, shows a permanent collection of established contemporary artists (Dali, Carnou, Le Grec), and offers numbered editions of books on art as well as lithographs.

The **Librairie du Cygne** is a serious bookstore that specializes in books on art forms. Works on Wedgewood, Worcester, and Meissen were in the window when we looked.

Here in the small but neat **Galerie Bonaparte** you can find M. Zarakian, who exhibits paintings of the famous and future famous.

No. 13. Mme. Juliot collects eighteenth-century antiques, while at **No. 7,** farther up the street, M. Moinot collects the seventeenth century. Both have been here for decades and can show you fine signed pieces.

You are now at the intersection of the Rue Bonaparte and the Rue des Beaux Arts. If you wish to take the time to see a beautifully appointed hotel, called simply L'Hôtel, walk a few steps down to the right. Wander in all the way to the back of the reception rooms, where there are bowers of plants and a parrot flying free.

Continue down the Rue Bonaparte to **Veranda,** No. 11. A translation of their own card is the best description possible. "Baroque Attractions—Exotic Charms—The Veranda, a boutique near the Beaux-Arts has collected home ornaments, unexpected furniture, paintings of 'genre' and story, objects of lighting and curiosity, what you would like to offer or receive. Annick Clavier and Jean Ollivary having united their enthusiasms and put the Past into the Present await you at the Veranda." Jean Ollivary, an antique dealer, decorated a salon for Annick Clavier, and from that collaboration developed the idea to open this most attractive shop. You might find old bakers' racks, for bread and pastry, a single school desk for three pupils, or a fine selection of still-life paintings.

Backyard of the Comoglio Antique Store

No. 7. R.G. is a master picture-framer who has been selling reproductions of the finest old frames for 35 years.

No. 3. London Studios are the exclusive importers from Portobello Road of reproductions of English furniture and marine paintings on glass. The French love English furniture. Don't we all!

No. 1. Josephine, of Napoleon fame, is a storehouse of the best and finest silver that has ever been made.

Before crossing the Rue Bonaparte to continue this walk we do want to tell you what lies at the end of this street. You reach the Quai Malaquais, and the Institute of France, home of the French Academy, where the renowned dictionary writers and protectors of the purity of the French language work. Across the quai there is a footbridge over the Seine to the Louvre.

No. 2. The little low house across the street, with dormer windows and hook and reel for loading above it, was built in 1620. This site was originally a Brothers of Charity hospital until Queen Margot forced them out in order to build her neighborhood estate. The Paris American Art is a huge art supply store serving the Ecole des Beaux Arts, the school of fine arts down the street. The shop was started at the turn of the century by an American.

At **No. 8,** Felix M. has collected some of the best and most beautiful pieces of Art Déco and Art Nouveau that we have ever seen. They are few but extremely fine.

At **No. 12,** M. Roux-Devillas spends his days surrounded by memories of the past. He specializes in old books, old documents (autographs), and old scientific instruments. The collection ranges from sun dials and eighteenth-century dental tools to treaties signed by kings. One home inventory of the wife of a French Lieutenant General in Martinique in 1791 divided her possessions into three sections: furnishings, silver, and slaves. All the slaves were identified and described in the same way: name, job, age, and price. There was Jurançon who took care of the boats, 32 years old, and worth 3300 pounds; Caroline, 5 years old, worth 500 pounds, no duties; and Lucille, who was too old and incapacitated to do or be worth anything at all, but was listed simply to note her existence, *"laissée pour mémoire."* Documents of this kind form the basis of historical research on slavery today. This was one of the few stores that offered valuable items of past history at reasonable rates.

Galerie Mai, also at No. 12, is a modern furniture store worth looking at because 20 years ago the owners decided to abandon "Danish modern" and represent contemporary artists and furniture designers. Pierre Lebe, one of their finds, is a versatile man who sculpts in stone, designs tapestries, and makes furniture and ceramics. He is faithful to the natural earth colors of brown, grey, white, and black, which he uses in all of his work. There are handsome coffee tables here made of black slate and rosewood.

No. 14—Ecole des Beaux Arts. This site is a ministage for the history of Paris. The first record of inhabitants dates from 1603 when Marie de Médicis, Henry IV's Italian wife, brought five priests from Florence and built for them, here, a charity hospital. These priests were not only Italian, they were surgeons and pharmacists. Clearly Marie de Médicis felt she needed more than serving ladies to accompany her to her new country and established, in effect, for her use as well as others, an Italian hospital and an Italian drugstore. (All these precautions bear a close resemblance to the American Hospital and the American Drugstore.) The Brothers of Charity Hospital moved three years later to the Rues des Sts. Pères and Jacob, where it became a large and important hospital, lasting until 1937 when it was eventually taken down.

After the removal of the original hospital, the eccentric Margot built her promised altar to Jacob here. Although the singing of nonstop litanies by the monks was stopped after five years, the convent remained until the Revolution, at which time it was forced to close down. It was left abandoned, but not for long.

During the French Revolution it was the sworn duty of each citizen to remove every symbol of religion and royalty he could find. A young painter and critic, Alexandre Lenoir, was quick to see the threat of destruction by the mad mob of all the art treasures and manuscripts in Paris. After eloquent and anguished pleading, he received permission to take or buy all the treasures he could find, to store the books and manuscripts in two other convents, and to store the art treasures in this one. There followed frenzied years of snatching books from fire, saving statues of precious metal from the mint, and rescuing kings from their coffins at St. Denis. A bayonet pierced Lenoir when he threw himself upon Richelieu's tomb in the church of the Sorbonne to save it from the mob. He was unable to save the row of statues under the first balcony of Notre Dame (the

one in *The Hunchback of Notre Dame* on which the beggars climbed
to save Esmeralda from the hands of the Hunchback.) These
statues, meant to represent the kings of the Old Testament,
but done in the anachronistic style of Merovingian kings, were
taken to be kings of France and smashed—each and every one
of them. But Lenoir got whatever he could, however he could,
and gathered it in, until this old convent was such a storehouse
as had never been seen before and will never be seen again.

When the Terror was over, Lenoir could stand back and look
at the most eloquent creations of eighteen centuries of French
art. He was inspired to make this cave of Ali Baba into a
museum of French monuments. In 1795 it became a reality.
Chroniclers describe the display of treasures as the most
beautiful and impressive ever gathered in one place. It lasted
through the Directory, 1795-1799, through the Consulate,
1799-1804, and the Empire, 1807-1812. Napoleon, in his zeal to
preserve the glory of France, showered gifts and privileges on
it. Perhaps that is the real reason for the present name of the
street. But Louis XVIII made the irresponsible decision, one of
many, of closing the museum and dispersing its contents. He
allowed each locality to claim the return of their old art
treasures.

Although the museum was disbanded, it has reappeared in the
sixteenth arrondissement at the Place de Trocadèro as the
Museum of French Monuments, with copies (magnificently
done copies) of religious art throughout France. This
monastery was then turned into a school of fine arts, the Ecole
des Beaux Arts, or just Beaux Arts as it is familiarly called.

Pass the pile of motorcyles as you enter the courtyard, and in
honor of Alexandre Lenoir look first at his statue to your right
between the columns of a chapel doorway. His face is dirty, the
pediment is broken, his name is hardly legible. The history
books heap generous praise on him, as we have done; the
government won't spend a cent to restore him.

The odd remains of château doors and pieces of sculpture that
decorate the courtyard are all classified historic monuments.
Not so for the atrocious modern building stuck onto the back of
the archways facing the entry. You may not see it at first
glance (probably a builder's attempt at concealment), but look
again. In back of this poor construction is the classic and
original building put up in 1858, when the school was opened.
Enter the building on the Seine side, and look into the work

studios. Most of the students are pleased to show you what they are doing. We passed through studios of wood and metal, mosaic and stone, and plaster and paper.

Continue through the building until you come to the delightful Cour du Mûrier (the court of the mulberry tree), which was a cloister of the convent. If the weather permits, sit on the grass (a good spot for lunch), look around, and listen. The empty pedestals in each cloister bay once were capped by pieces of sculpture that had won the Grand Prize of Rome. This coveted prize allowed the winner to go to Rome to study the antique and Renaissance masters in the Villa Médicis. Critics claimed, however, that as long as the best talent got training such as this, French art was likely to remain classical. The absence of sculpture in this courtyard makes the decline of Italian influence all too clear, and listening and speaking to the students makes it even clearer. They did not even know why the pedestals were bare, nor what had been there before. We made other inquiries about the school and could get no information, until a young girl said the students knew nothing about the place, really, and that we should ask for a guide in the office. By this time the patched and graffitied walls, the missing sculpture, and the ignorance of the students made us suspicious, and we marched into the office requesting a guide. As we graduated from counters to offices we began to figure out the mystery. We were told that because of the great deal of work going on since the "events" (that is, the student strikes) of 1968 (we saw no work going on—ever) there were no guided tours. There is and will be no brochure to tell anything about the school. A secretary assured us we were not receiving different treatment from others. She had hundreds of letters of requests in her files; the director refused every one.

We left in search of students, who did finally answer some of our questions. It turns out that the students at Beaux Arts were among the most disruptive in the revolt of 1968, and they destroyed and damaged a good deal of the school. At that time the school granted all sorts of student demands, including one to separate the faculties for painting, architecture, sculpture, etc., in order to improve the level of teaching, which the students felt was too general. The administration, cleverly, has continued this idea of division to such a degree that it has weakened the communal role of the students. Classes are held all over Paris, painters never see sculptors, and even the famous costume ball of the Beaux Arts has not been held since the uprising. The only group activity is political; the first courtyard is filled with screaming posters about injustice everywhere.

And then we learned that the school looks so neglected because in five years it will be turned into a museum of Renaissance art. Then the Beaux Arts will be scattered in smaller buildings all over Paris. No one seems to care very much. What a pity!

We were sitting on a stone ledge in the big courtyard on the Quai Malaquais, wondering where the spirit of art students had gone, when we were suddenly doused with cold water from a balcony above. Amid the hilarious gales of laughter on the part of the perpetrators of this prank, we were told how lucky we were it wasn't ink, paint, or clay

Below, **Boulakia** exhibits twentieth-century art. Also here, **Sala** has a selection of amazing pieces of seventeenth-century furniture.

No. 20 is another spot that marks this area as Henry IV's. Of all his women, Gabrielle d'Estrée is the one he loved most, and in the back of this courtyard is a house in which their son, César de Vendôme, once abbé of St. Germain, lived. He was born illegitimate in 1594, recognized the following year, and would have been king had Louis XIII not been born.

No. 26. Fabrice is one of the three fantasy shops of the same name, specializing in ivory, wood, and amber oddments and jewelry. The shop is famous for bracelets made from the thick bristle of an elephant's tail and considered by the French a good-luck charm.

No. 28. Le Petit Faune, the small children's clothing store, sells high-style clothes, expensive even when on sale. The safety pin as doorknob looks inviting, but the ladies who run the store specialize in a kind of impatience one finds too often in Paris.

Le Mur du Nomade has its entrance on the Rue Jacob. The nomad's wall is, of course, tapestry hung. These hangings are completely French, from Renaissance reproductions to Lurçat (the reviver of tapestry art today), to contemporary artists like Arp and Picart-le-Doux. Whether or not tapestries interest you, go into this shop to watch the young man who is weaving a tapestry on a loom exactly as it was done hundreds of years ago at the Aubusson factory. Today, Aubusson is still France's national school and factory for tapestry-weaving and rug-making—the only place one can be trained for this work. School is followed by three years as an apprentice and then five more years before the weaver is permitted to work alone. Tapestries that are woven at Aubusson sell here, the price depending on size and the fame of the artist. Eight copies of a design are made, six for sale, one or two for the artist. Less expensive "walls of wool" as Le Corbusier called them, can be purchased here also, for example, an artisanal tapestry, woven wool on which a picture is printed. The shop has rooms in the back and upstairs; the people here are most helpful and instructive.

Apart from several bookstores and a jeweler, this next section of Rue Bonaparte (between Rue Jacob and Rue l'Abbaye) seems to belong to **Nobilis,** specialists in wall covering and materials for the home. They occupy Nos. 29, 31, 32, 34, 38, and 40, but No. 34 is the door to enter for fast service by experienced and devoted sales people.

We are now back to our starting point—St. Germain des Prés. If you have already visited the church let us move directly ahead to the boulevard for a table at the famous café, Les Deux Magots, or its rival, the Flore.

You are now in the heart of what was and to some extent still is, the artistic and literary center of Paris. Before World War I Picasso and Apollinaire were already installed at the Flore, in back, although they were also habitués of the even more popular cafés of Montparnasse: the Dôme, the Rotonde, and the Closeries des Lilas. How many cafés can one frequent? When did they work, and where did they work?

The "lost generation" of expatriates after World War I, some of whom drank themselves into oblivion, frequented both St. Germain and Montparnasse. One distinction, however, between the two areas seems to be that students favored St. Germain des Prés, and artists, Montparnasse. Reread Hemingway's *A Moveable Feast* and *The Sun Also Rises* for the feel of these days gone by.

Les Deux Magots was the birthplace of surrealism, the Café Flore the home of the existentialists. Simone de Beauvoir and Sartre had their regular table at the latter, drawing all the young intellectuals like a magnet. Camus came, but not often, because Sartre was supposedly jealous of Camus; at any rate the two did not get along.

Today café life is still a scene to watch. The talk is at once stereotyped and unbelievable. Most of our eavesdropping brought forth information about ex-husbands and weekend houses or business deals concerning art, movies, and books. Most of the publishing houses have offices in this *quartier,* so that a constant stream of intellectuals will be around for a lunch or a drink. The younger crowd looks as if it were literally picked up whole from the wealthy sixteenth arrondissement and dropped into the cafés. One February night—granted, it was cold—we counted 27 fur coats on men in their early twenties or younger. Tourists come to look at everyone else; the French come to be looked at. It is still true that many of these people know each other, and the neighborhood keeps the character of a small town.

These cafés got their odd names the same way so many other places and streets in Paris did. The Deux Magots was the name of a novelty shop that planned to move to this spot from the Rue de Buci in 1873, but before that actually happened, a bar opened, used their name, and has been here ever since. The *deux magots* are the two wooden statues, inside the café on the central pillar, of Chinese dignitaries (most often portrayed in porcelain) that were to be the standard of the novelty shop. A small statue of Flora (goddess of flowers and mother of spring) used to stand at the door of the Café Flore. There is an interesting room on the second floor of the Flore decorated, as the French say, "in the English style."

Le Drugstore across the street will give you a hamburger or ice cream, but somehow these seem more French than American. Even the idea of calling the shop a "drugstore" is out of date. The drugstore as "hang-out" faded in the United States almost 20 years ago, but the translation of one country's mores into another's always lags. For example, Americans flaunt French ice cream and French dry cleaning as great luxuries for those who know. Any one who has spent any time in Paris knows that one piles up the dirty clothes to dry clean at home, and that the tiny balls of ice cream at high prices hardly resemble the real thing. Crêpes and fried potatoes in the French style, on the other hand, are well worth copying. Le Drugstore is one of the new mind-blowing spots with moving lights, changing decors, and steps leading up and down and around. A good bookstand and the arrival of the Paris *Herald* at midnight keeps the place packed.

A writer and filmmaker friend, Georges Perec (author of *Les Choses*), and others like him don't come to St. Germain anymore. But they still frequent small cafés off the beaten path. To Perec, cafés are not only an important part of his dreams, about which he writes, but the place where literature is made. Even if you don't make movies or write books, a regular table at a café of your choice is a great idea. You will find the same people coming back, and the owners of these little cafés in your neighborhood (if you are lucky enough to be here long enough to have one) are fascinating people. Besides, these are the traditional spots for letter-writing as a daytime occupation. In the old days you would be supplied with writing paper, ink, and a quill pen.

Two restaurants, almost within sight of the square, that are "worth the trip" are Lipp and Vagenende.

Lipp, No. 15 Blvd. St. Germain, is a restaurant that has done what we would have considered the impossible. The French, as you know, consider themselves the arbiter of fine taste, and the country they might least copy would be Germany. The namesake of the restaurant, Lippmann, was an Alsatian and desperately unhappy about the separation of his home from France. The food and drink he served, however, was totally German: frankfurters and sauerkraut, light and dark beer. The amazing fact is that this dish caught on, that it appears today on almost every Parisian menu, is sold fresh in every *charcuterie*, in cans in every grocery, and is now the *raison d'être* of hundreds of restaurants in Paris.

In the early 1900s Lipp was the after-theater place to dine, as the Plaza Athenée was 20 years ago. The lovely ladies shown in engravings, picking up their long dresses as they stepped from horse-driven hacks, were no doubt going to dine at Lipp. By 1924 the area had become so much the *quartier* of editors (two steps to Grosset, four to Gallimard, and six to Hachette) and their prize-winning writers, that Lipp was forced to enlarge— not like the Deux Magots who could extend its stomach onto the sidewalk—but by turning and twisting into the recesses behind the restaurant. In the 1960s Lipp was the eating place for politicians as well as writers. François Mitterand, chief of the French Socialist party, used to dine here, perhaps still does. Ben Barka, a Moroccan militant, was arrested here.

The food is fine, but we are sorry to report that this is the only restaurant that refused to give us a recipe—the one for frankfurters and sauerkraut and surely not the most prized one in Paris.

Vagenende, No. 142, is a joy to behold. Here is 1900 in all its fantasy and variety. You will see many a floral door on the Blvd. St. Germain, but they are a product of the 1970s. This restaurant and the even more fantastic restaurant of the Gare de Lyons (that was shown in the film *Travels with My Aunt*) are the real thing, built when the creation of Art Nouveau was at its height. We tried to buy one of the side servers from the Vagenende. The proprietor smiled condescendingly and informed us she could have sold it 50 times over. Rivaling the restaurant's wonderful appearance is the food itself. The fare is French, and the price is low. We wonder how this restaurant can serve a four-course dinner or a variety of other dishes for so little. Go early (at 12 or before 8), if you don't reserve in advance. An accordionist or a violinist will entertain you at dinner.

Although you have walked and talked and looked for a good

two hours, these few streets are only a sample of what the neighborhood has to offer. It is no doubt time, however, to sit down at a café or restaurant and restore yourself. Bon Appetit!

Mouffetard

METRO: Censier Daubenton, Monge

BUS: No. 47

STREETS: Rue Mouffetard, Rue l'Arbalète, Rue des Patriarches, Place des Patriarches, Place Contrescarpe, Rue Blainville, Rue Descartes

De par le roi, défense à Dieu
De faire miracle en ce lieu.

By order of the king, God is forbidden
To perform miracles in this place.

The Rue Mouffetard is different from our other walks because,
although it is one of the liveliest streets in Paris and has a
fascinating history behind it, many of the events that
happened here have left no traces in this market street. We
recommend that you read this walk beforehand so that you
won't be trying to read while you're being jostled by the crowds
of shoppers. This will also allow you to spend your time
discovering the pleasures of the *marché* for yourself. If you don't
read this before you go to Mouffetard, begin by sitting in the
garden of the church of St. Médard before you venture into the
market. After you have left this garden, you will be unable to
find a place to sit other than cafés and curbs.

There are three good times of the day to come and visit this
neighborhood: The best is between 9 a.m. and noon, particularly on a Saturday or Sunday, when you can see the most
colorful outdoor food market in Paris; the second is in the
afternoon, when the crowds have gone home and the buildings
become visible once more; and the third is at night, when all the
restaurants and cafés are open and the youth of Paris (and the
tourists) are out to eat and people-watch.

In ancient times the Rue Mouffetard was important as the
main Roman road to the southeast, Lyons, and Italy, but it owes
its real development to the Bièvre River. This river flowed
across the base of the hill where the street ends today (originally

the road continued to the Porte d'Italie). Its banks offered excellent land for settlement, and in the twelfth century the area, called the Bourg St. Marcel, was a village where wealthy Parisians had farms and country houses. The list of residents of the midfourteenth century reads like the social register. In a huge area (presently defined by three streets, Mouffetard, Lacépède, and Geoffroy St. Hilaire, and the Bièvre River) there were only two roads, Mouffetard and Daubenton, and apart from the church, only seven estates. They were owned by bishops, lords, the president of the courts, and Charles V's architect.

Nevertheless, the dominance of the upper class was not long lasting, again because of the Bièvre. The river ran with sweet water, which encouraged cultivation and was famous for its fresh-water shrimp, described by Madame de Maintenon as "the best that could be imagined." However, the river was soon discovered to contain properties efficacious in skinning and tanning hides. Rabelais offers a delightful explanation for this phenomenon in *Pantagruel*, Book II, Chapter XXII. In this story Panurge takes revenge on the finest lady in town, who had scorned his love. He kills a bitch in heat and carefully prepares "that part [about which] the Greek necromancers knew." The following day was a feast day, and, finding the woman in her best clothes in the church,

. . . Panurge deftly sprinkled the drug that he was carrying onto various parts of her, chiefly on the pleats of her sleeves and her dress. . . . All the dogs in the church ran up to the lady, attracted by the smell of the drug he had sprinkled on her. Small and great, big and little, all came, lifting their legs, smelling her and pissing all over her. It was the most dreadful thing in the world. . . . Panurge made a show of driving them off. Then took leave of her and retired into a chapel to see the fun. For these beastly dogs pissed over all her clothes, a great greyhound wetting on her head, others on her sleeves, on her shoes; so that all the women who were thereabouts had great difficulty in saving her. . . .

At this Panurge burst out laughing, and said to some of the gentlemen of the city, "I think that woman's on heat [sic], or else she has recently been covered by a greyhound."

And when he saw all the dogs snorting around her as they do round a hot bitch, he went off to fetch Pantagruel. Everywhere on the way, when he saw a dog, he gave it a kick and said, "Aren't you going to join your mates at the wedding? Get on, get on, devil take you! Get along with you now!"

Then, having got to their lodging, he said to Pantagruel: "Master, I beg of you come and see all the dogs, come and see all the dogs of this land, flocking round a lady. She is the most beautiful lady in the town, and they want to roger her."

Pantagruel very gladly accepted this invitation and went to see the show, which he found very fine and original. But the best of it all was the procession, in which more than 600,014 dogs were seen all around her, bothering her greatly, and everywhere she passed fresh hosts of dogs followed her trail, pissing in the road where her gown had touched it.

Everyone stopped to see the show, gazing with admiration at the dogs, who leapt as high as her neck and spoiled all her fine clothes. For this she could find no other remedy but to retire into her mansion. So she ran to hide, with the dogs after her and all the chambermaids laughing. But once she was inside and the door closed behind her, all the dogs ran up from two miles around and pissed so hard against the gate of the house, that they made a stream with their urine big enough for ducks to swim in. And it is this stream which now passes by St. Victor, in which Mme. Gobelin dyes her scarlet, thanks to the specific virtue of those piss-hounds, as our master Dungpowder once proclaimed in a public sermon.

In the sixteenth and seventeenth centuries the population of the Bourg St. Marcel became working class, made up of tanners, slaughterers, skinners, dyers, and similar craftsmen. They named their bridge that crossed the river, the Pont aux Tripes, (tripe bridge). The famous Gobelins wool factory is the only survivor from this period. It was because of the Flemish tapestry weavers at the Gobelins that the second characteristic of the neighborhood developed. The Flemish were great beer drinkers, a tradition they would not leave behind, and soon cafés and cabarets proliferated to serve them. The successors of these establishments are still there.

Industry, particularly the rotting animal wastes, rapidly polluted the purity of the Bièvre. By the nineteenth century this neighborhood was the commercial and shopping center of the Left Bank, but the fumes from the Bièvre were more noxious than ever. There is a theory that the name of the Rue Mouffetard comes from these sewerlike qualities of the river: The French for skunk or bad smell is *moufettes*. (There is also a less amusing explanation that claims that the hill was called in Roman times *mons cetardus*, perhaps named after a now forgotten Roman, which became *mont cetard*, then *montfetard*, and finally *Mouffetard*.) In 1828 a portion of the river was covered, in 1840-

48 studies were done to try and save the Bièvre, but in 1910 the only possible solution finally came to pass: The river became part of the underground sewer system. In the summer, today, on certain corners, the foul odor of garbage still seems to emanate from the pavement under your feet.

CHURCH OF ST. MEDARD

The door to the church of St. Médard faces the market on the Rue Mouffetard. Architecturally, this church is not particularly notable, though some of the events connected with it are. The first church on this spot is thought to have been built in the seventh or eighth century, in dedication to St. Médard, but there is no evidence to support this theory. The first positive proof of the existence of this church is in a papal bull of Pope Alexander III. It dates from 1163, when the Pope came to Paris to consecrate the choir of St. Germain des Prés and to lay the first stone for Notre Dame. This bull mentions, under the rights and lands of the Abbey Ste. Geneviève, the Bourg St. Marcel and a church, St. Médard, on the left bank of the Bièvre. There are no physical traces of this church except for the bell tower, since renovated, which was originally separate from the body of the then much smaller church. The actual building is from several periods. The nave and the facade, in flamboyant Gothic, are from the middle fifteenth century. The money for their construction probably came from a donation from the sister of Reilhac, the lawyer of King Charles VII. She wanted the priests to say 261 low masses a year for her brother, who was buried there. In 1736, 200 years later, the priests had cut this down to 16; today there is no one to remember him.

In 1560-86 the choir was enlarged and chapels rebuilt in the style of the Renaissance. The windows of the nave are also from this period. The money this time came from fines imposed on Protestants after a religious battle. The money ran out at the vaulted ceiling, however, and so it had to be completed in wood. It remains wood to this day, a refreshing change from stone vaulting. In 1665 the side aisles were added, although the vaulting, which had served as buttressing for the church, is earlier (sixteenth century). In the eighteenth century the church was again redone to fit the existing fashions. The columns are fluted in the neoclassical style, and the apsidal Chapel of the Virgin, behind the choir, was built. The walls are completely covered with votive tablets that give thanks for miraculous recoveries, exams passed, and life in general. During the Revolution the church was made into a temple of labor—a citizen's meeting place—and the standard still hangs over the choir. In 1901 the *petit charnier*, a small roomlike enclosure for common graves located behind the church, was condemned and transformed into the catechism chapel. In this and other chapels there are some interesting paintings—note "The Merchants Being Chased from the Temple" by Matoire and the "Multiplication of the Bread" by Restout. In the last left-hand chapel (with your back to the entrance) is a painting of Ste. Geneviève that was at one time thought to be by Watteau.

Take a seat in a lit area, and read up to the section marked Rue Mouffetard.

Outside the church was once the cemetery of St. Médard. Originally, it included the area in front of the church, where the square now is, and the entire left side back to what is now the Rue Censier. At the beginning of each winter, before the ground froze, a large ditch was dug that served as a common grave for all who died during the winter. It was closed in the spring, and several smaller ones were dug to take the few summer dead. (In primitive conditions on the margin of subsistence, the winter months were always far more deadly than the summer, if only because the poor could not get enough food to keep warm and sustain resistance to disease. The combination of the Bièvre and the rotting corpses must have been overwhelming.) The church buried about 300 people a year in this fashion. After nine years they would reuse a large ditch and after three or four, the smaller ones. When the Rue Censier was opened in 1913, a layer of bones 24 inches thick was uncovered 10 feet down. A coin found among the bones dates them from the 1590s.

In 1765 a law was passed forbidding any burials within the limits of the city. The people of the neighborhood had no desire to be buried at Ste. Catherine, which was far away, so with the complicity of the old beadles, who had the cemetery keys in their safe keeping, they continued to be buried at St. Médard in secrecy. This went on through the Revolution, until the police, in 1795, became indignant about this *"manie de perpetuer l'ancien régime"* (this nonsense of perpetuating the old regime).

The most famous corpse of St. Médard was a young Jansenist, François Pâris. He was a novice with a great reputation for humility. He preferred to spend his life performing menial tasks, such as knitting socks for the poor, and he died at the age of 36 on May 1, 1727, at the height of the Jansenist persecution, exhausted from a life of extreme abstinence and self-punishment. Pâris was buried with the poor in the *charnier*, having insisted before he died that he was not worthy of the cemetery. The Jansenists declared him a saint, and a black marble stone was laid over his tomb. The grave soon became a gathering place for his admirers, and before long the word spread that the site was holy and capable of miraculous cures. This was the beginning of an unbelievable history of mass hysteria that lasted 35 years. Young girls, fanatics, began coming to the *charnier* to eat the dirt of the novice priest's grave. There they would fall into religious ecstasies or convulsions and have to be restrained. At first there were 8 to 10 girls, but after two years the number had risen to 800. The girls' activities escalated from day to day, changing from mere convulsions to atrocities. They would ask to be beaten while crying out, "Oh! How good that is. Oh! How good that makes me feel, brother. I beg of you, continue if you can!" They wanted to have their tongues pierced, 25-pound weights placed upon their chests,

their bodies raked with iron combs, or their breasts, thighs, and stomachs trampled on until they fainted. Pain was voluptuous, and it had no bounds. They had their breasts crushed or were hung head down. Some girls had themselves tortured in this way more than 20 times.

On January 27, 1732, the government in desperation had the cemetery walled, locked, and guarded. The next day at St. Médard, on the locked gate, the following rhyme appeared:

> De par le roi, défense à Dieu
> De faire miracle in ce lieu.

> By order of the king, God is forbidden
> To perform miracles in this place.

The girls had to move their activities to private houses—the tomb of the novice priest was no longer necessary. In fact, in March 1733 another law was vainly passed, forbidding all those seized by convulsions to turn their affliction into a public spectacle or to arrange meetings for this purpose in private houses. Some girls were imprisoned on these grounds, but this only made the others more impassioned and caused some of the most unusual scenes to occur. The girls borrowed an idea from ancient Miletus and began strangling themselves; they also swallowed live coals and leatherbound editions of the New Testament. Sister Rosalie, we are told, lived for 40 days, on air sipped from a spoon, and one girl had herself nailed to a board and was thus crucified.

In direct association with the ecstatics were the *mélangistes*, who pretended to distinguish between useless, indecent acts and true religious ecstasy. The *sécouristes* were those who gave aid to the convulsive girls. They gave small aid and big aid. Small aid consisted of helping to prevent falls and other accidents and of helping to defend the girls' modesty by rearranging their often disordered clothing. Big or "murderous" aid entailed inflicting all the forms of martyrdom that the girls would beg for.

Not everyone was so helpful. In a convent near St. Médard the nuns would miaow in unison for several hours every day at the same time. It was a disturbance, and the neighbors were up in arms. The nuns were told if one more noise was heard from their convent, the Garde Française, which was posted at their gate, would come in and whip them. There was complete silence.

This Jansenist cult continued at the same frenetic rate for 35 years until August 1762, when the Jesuit society that had, with the help of the government, persecuted them for so long, was disbanded and expelled from the country. As for the girls, as French historian J. Dulaure points out, if a girl is brought up by people who believe in possession of the soul by the devil, and the girl herself believes this, she is bound to become very anxious at a certain age about new and unavowable emotions that seem to be tormenting her. She finds it easy to believe she has become possessed. Dulaure also offers another explanation: If a girl has been reared by very devout people and is herself religious, her own devotions and abstinences may continue increasing until she reaches a point of religious ecstasy. In her case it is love that has taken a wrong turn. Dulaure alludes only in passing to the explanation that we today might find most plausible, namely, that this was a search for a form of sexual release acceptable to the religious and social milieu of the day.

In 1807 Pâris's tomb was opened in order to give certain eminent Jansenist families relics of this saint; the rest of his bones lie under what are now the unmarked stones of the Chapel of the Virgin.

St. Médard has also played a small role in literature. Old fans of Victor Hugo's *Les Miserables* will remember, perhaps, that it was here that Jean Valjean accidentally encountered Javert. There was always a beggar by St. Médard, posted under the street lamp, to whom Jean gave a few sous. One evening the beggar lifts his head briefly to look at Jean under the light. Jean shivers with fear, for he is certain that he has seen the face of his enemy, Javert, and not the old beggar.

Today, the beggar is no longer there, although one evening we were lucky enough to come across some living art at his old stand. It was just before Christmas, and the street was strung with lights and crowded with shoppers at the market. In front of the church three young people were performing a short play in mime. It was the classic story of the doll-girl who is brought to life when she finally receives attention and love. We felt as if we had returned to the Middle Ages and were watching a mummers' play in front of some old cathedral. What did disappoint us, though, was the way in which the vast majority of the spectators ungraciously left as soon as the hat was passed. And while the fact and manner of the performance definitely conveyed a medieval flavor, the players didn't. There was

something in their easy manner and their willingness to
perform publicly not often found among the French. When we
paused to commiserate with them over their small earnings
our suspicions were confirmed—they were Americans trying to
earn a little money.

THE MARKET

Today the *marché* stretches out from the Carrefour des
Gobelins, which is not on our walk, to the Rue l'Epée de Bois
and spreads right and left almost a block on each side street.
The scholars tell us there has been a street market in this area
since 1350, and it is this that forms the character of the street.
The origins of the market, however, are a bit disquieting. We are
told that, in the fourteenth century, on the Ile de la Cité under
the shadow of Notre Dame, there was a butcher who sold the
finest pâté in Paris. One day, however, his unusual sources of
new material were discovered; the meat used in his excellent
pâté was human flesh. The butcher and his friend the barber
had been abducting students who lived under the auspices of the
church (away from their families) and were killing them behind
the barber shop. These poor youths, living anonymously among
the crowds of students, were not missed until the day the
barber picked out a young man who owned a dog. When his
master did not return from the barber, the dog put up such a
howl that the youth's friends came to investigate and caught the
barber and the butcher in their bloody work. Judgment was
swift: The two men were suspended in cages in front of Notre
Dame and publicly burned. The clerics of the cathedral,
however, were in a more ambiguous position. The well-fed
priests had long enjoyed this pâté, but to eat human flesh, even
unknowingly, is the sin of anthropophagy, and is punishable by
excommunication. Several of the priests of Notre Dame,
therefore, had to be exiled from their cathedral. They banded
together in their exclusion and decided that to plead their
cause and beg forgiveness they would make a pilgrimage to the
Pope in Avignon. They set out barefoot one morning on the
road to the southeast. They arrived 20 minutes later, at what is
now the Carrefour des Gobelins (then just outside the city
limits). There they decided that their feet hurt enough and that
they should stop at that very spot and become mendicants.
They lived from their begging until later in that same year when
Jean de Meulan, the new Bishop of Paris, came to visit his

property and farms on the hill of Mouffetard. During his visit he was attacked by thieves and would have been killed if not for the aid of the mendicant priests. In appreciation, Jean de Meulan gave the priests absolution and, taking account of their record, allowed them to open a market on his property to sell "*toutes marchandises et objets dont on n'aurait pas à rechercher l'origine*" (all goods and objects of unquestionable origin).

Again, there are official records in 1654 of a vegetable market held every Wednesday and Friday in the courtyard of the Maison du Patriarche, then owned by the family of the Maréchal Biron. An ordinance of September 20, 1828, authorized the clearing of this site, and the architect, Châtillon, was given a commission to build a covered market in place of the house. It was inaugurated on June 1, 1831. At that time the market sold primarily old clothes and ironwork, with only a small section for food. The actual building was later used as a garage and is presently occupied by public baths.

The street market we see today is devoted almost exclusively to food. It's an interesting and especially nice *marché*, because unlike the peripatetic markets assembled from temporary stands, which are set up in a given street two òr three mornings a week, Mouffetard consists almost entirely of permanent shops that lay out their goods daily, covering the sidewalk. This is much closer to the medieval system, in which each store had a large horizontally split shutter that was opened for selling. The top half would be a shade to protect against the sun and the rain, and the bottom would be used as a table on which to display the goods. Hanging out past the shutters would be the man's standard with a symbol representing the shop's name, which in itself was symbolic of the business. The room behind this street front was used for storage, or, if the shop were owned by a craftsman, he would use the room as his workshop. Although the shutters are gone, and the displays are richer than in the Middle Ages, the room behind is still used to store the crates of vegetables and fruits; in some cases (the butchers and fishmongers) it has become part of the store. The array at the *marché*, particularly on Sunday morning, is dazzling. There are heaps of every fresh vegetable and fruit in season, plus two stands of exotic fruits. Some of these are available and common in the United States—mangoes, plaintains, papaya—but some we had never seen nor heard of. These stands also sell all varieties of glossy, sensuous peppers with the full range of greens, reds, and whites thrown together in baskets and boxes; melons; fresh unpeeled almonds; and cranberries, an essentially unknown fruit in France and one we saw only here and in Fauchon in the Place de la Madeleine. (Fauchon is an extraordinarily fine supermarket similar to Fortnum and Mason's in London, except that in Paris gastronomic and esthetic beauty have been combined. It is worth visiting, but don't expect to buy unless you can print money. The prices are astronomical.) The special fruit stands are on the Rue des Patriarches and at the square right in front of St. Médard. This stand in the square is the most beautiful one in the *marché*. The display is marvelous, and the colors and shapes are staggering. We spoke with the people who own the stand. They told us that it is run completely by the family, as are most shops in France. They start work daily at 4 a.m., when they first buy their goods from the central market, *les halles,* in Rungis, and then come to Paris to set up and begin selling from nine until seven in the evening with only Monday off. They also told us that many of their customers were restaurant owners, and when we asked if it was a profitable business, the little girl nodded her head "yes" vigorously, and her mother blushingly agreed. The majority of the stalls at the *marché* sell more common produce. Take the time to walk around, comparing quality and prices. We ended up shopping from a different stand for almost each item—one man sold the cheapest carrots and onions, while another, the best apples and bananas. If you are staying in Paris for a long time and can shop, we know of no nicer way to feel French and a part of the city than to buy each type of food from your own favorite merchant. (Don't forget your shopping bag!) Patronizing your own carefully chosen bakery can be one of the most pleasant, as well as fattening, experiences. One of our personal recommendations is to be adventurous. Don't buy California Sunkist oranges when you can try, for less money, the Spanish *sanguines,* or blood oranges. Try all kinds of delicatessen salads and meats, including the ones you have been brought up to think are disgusting. Also try the cheeses. American cheddar is not available, so eat the many others. Contrary to popular belief the smell of a cheese does not necessarily indicate how strong it is at all. Chaume, a mild, creamy, sinful cheese, reeks. Avoid the supermarket versions of cheese; the cheese store sells the unpasteurized, truer version at lower prices. In general, be daring.

The Mouffetard market fulfills every food need possible, a reputation this street has had for a long time. August Vitu wrote about Mouffetard in the late nineteenth century:

There is an average of two stores in each building, and all of them are dedicated to the daily subsistence of a very large, very crowded population with little time to spare and a large appetite to satisfy. On the ground floor of the 142 houses on the Rue Mouffetard there are 52 wine merchants, plus 9 wine merchants who also cater food and roast meat—yours or their own—16 grocers, 8 butchers, 6 bakers, 6 dairies, 5 delicatessens, 5 pastry shops, 4 lemonade stands, 3 tripe butchers, 2 café-bars, 1 horse-meat butcher, 3 coal sellers, 1 coffee store. This, which could feed an entire city, was complemented by fish, fresh vegetables, fruits, and flowers sold from outdoor rolling carts. The housekeeping of the Rue Mouffetard is kept up by three stove and pottery stores, one bottle shop, two glaziers, two brushmen and shoe repair and tool stores, one lighting store, one wall-paper and business supply store. Between the butchers and delicatessens with their reddish tinge and the pastrymen and bakers with their crusty tidbits are six linen and sewing stores; eight shoemakers for men, women, and children; four umbrella shops; three hatmakers for men, three for the women; and four gift shops spilling their wares out into the street, closely followed by a launderer-stain remover. While five barbers are caring for the heads hatted by the hatters, two watch and jewelry stores represent luxury, two wash-it-yourself-by-hand laundries represent cleanliness, teamed with a bathtub and bathroom fixtures salesman. The health of the body is watched by a doctor, two pharmacists, two herboristeries, two dentists to whom are attached three midwives in case of need. There is an office for job placement, one post office, one barracks of the Garde Républicaine, (once the Garde Française) to guarantee security. For intellectual culture one finds on the street one kindergarten and one reading room. Even art has its representative in the person of a photographer.

To compare how the street has changed in 70 years, we recently did a count. There is a greater variety now and certain trades, like the wine shops, have greatly decreased, while others, like the restaurants, have practically taken over the street. Now, with only one store per building, we found five bakeries, eight butchers, and two tripe stores, seven "American-style" small supermarkets, five delicatessens, six fruit and vegetable stores, plus three more daily stands at the market, six fishmongers, three horse butchers, five wine shops, three cheese shops, one coffee and spice supplier, and one poultry shop. There are also 18 restaurants, 2 restaurant-discothèques, and 11 cafés at your service. For health and beauty there are 10 women's clothing stores, 2 for children, 2 for men, and 5 more for everyone together. There are two wool and baby clothes shops, one fabric store, one beauty parlor, four shoestores, one laundry, one lingerie shop, one perfume and cosmetics store, and three pharmacies. For your house: one coal distributor, two dish and hardware stores, one more for utensils, and three flower shops. To feed the mind and soul there is one church, two bookstores, one communal activities center, two theaters, two art galleries, and a kindergarten. Under the heading of miscellaneous come one souvenir stand, one watch and photography shop, one bank, one hotel, four small industries, and the same barracks of the Garde Républicaine that Vitu mentions.

An aspect of the street Vitu didn't see in his day is the construction and renovation that is so common now. Whole blocks of eighteenth-century construction have been condemned—one has already been torn down for old people's housing. Asked about the destruction, any old-timer will shake his head and mourn the changes in the neighborhood, "It's just not the same, the atmosphere has changed." Although we were frustrated several times searching for vanished "historical" sites, for us, having come from the New World, the atmosphere and age are still palpable and exciting.

RUE MOUFFETARD

No. 134. As you walk up the Rue Mouffetard, take your time to look at the buildings and courtyards. The houses are almost all from the seventeenth century and are generally very plain with simple mansard windows and undecorated facades. They were built for ordinary people of modest means. No. 134 (to the left of No. 132—the number is not clearly marked), however, is very different. Its facade is extravagantly decorated with what appears to be twentieth-century work. On the second floor are panels of painted wood depicting country people at their tasks. (There are other panels similar to this on the bakery on the corner of the Rue des Patriarches and Mouffetard.) Above on the stucco is what we think is a unique scene showing wild game and birds intertwined with a floral pattern. Even the seventeenth-century mansard windows have been decorated.

We were not able to learn who installed these and when. The shop below is, appropriately, that of a butcher.

No. 122. This is decorated with the oldest standard remaining on the street, A la Bonne Source (at the good spring). Look above the doorway and notice the bas-relief of two boys, dressed in the style of Henry IV's reign, drawing water from a well. In 1592 this shop was owned by M. du Puy (the name means "of the well"), who sold wine and used the name of the shop as an implicit seal of approval. This type of pun as well as the link to the shop owner's name was typical of the play on words of medieval standards and necessary in a time without street numbers or the yellow pages.

Standards go back to the thirteenth century and beyond, when noblemen marked their houses with their coats of arms. If you were not a nobleman, you might distinguish your residence by placing a statuette of your favorite saint in a niche above the door. That way you got a little holy protection besides. Nos. 44 and 45 of the Rue Mouffetard still have niches in their facades, although the statues are long gone. The first commercial standards were put up by taverns and hotels, so that a foreigner could find a place to eat and sleep in a strange city. These standards generally represented a bundle of straw, which gives a good idea of the character of the sleeping accommodations.

The commercial standard was soon understood to be a smart way of advertising, and what was almost nonexistent in the thirteenth century had become a serious problem by the fifteenth. The standards were made from sheets of iron, cut and painted, and hung on long poles to extend into the street past the large shop shutters. Like signs today they were hung out as far as possible and made as large as possible to attract the most attention. Although Mouffetard has always been the same width that it is today, the combination of the shutters and an open sewer running down the center of the unpaved street—the whole overhung with huge groaning and clanking signs that blocked the sun—must have made for a dark and cluttered street. A *parfumerie* had a standard of a glove, each finger of which could have held a three-year-old child. A dentist hung a molar that was the size of an armchair. These standards were constantly threatening to fall—one man was reputedly killed when the dentist's tooth fell on his head. As in our time, though for reasons of safety rather than esthetics,

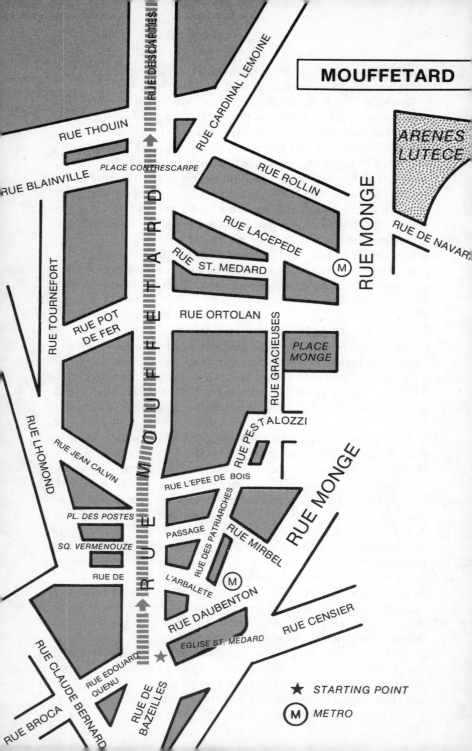

MOUFFETARD

the government tried to pass legislation to limit the size of signs. In 1667 they said the signs could be no more than 32 inches wide and had to be hung at least 15 feet above the ground, so that horsemen might ride in the streets comfortably. It was not until 1761 that standards were banned altogether, to be replaced by wall decorations like those at A la Bonne Source. A few of these decorations and old names still remain.

Not all signs designated the trade of the shop below so clearly as A la Bonne Source did. Since literacy was rare, the names were more often simply visual recognition or mnemonic devices—the kind of thing that would stick in your head. Actually this decorated house had previously been called The Bat, which tells us absolutely nothing. There are several old names that leave the business inside unexplained: The Bottle Tennis Court, or The Small Hole, or The Cage. Other names were clearer: The Tree of Life was a surgeon's house; The Red Shop, a butcher shop (the surgeon might have used that one too); The Reaper, a bakery (another possibility for the surgeon). One common name whose symbolism was clear in the Middle Ages was The Salamander. Salamanders were at that time believed to be impervious to fire, and therefore salamander was the old name for asbestos—the wood that wouldn't burn. Bakers often took this name to symbolize their clay baking ovens, and the word is still in use today for the ceramic room heaters commonly found in France.

Many of the names were religious, some specifically so: The Golden Cross, The White Cross, The Red Cross, The Name of Jesus, The Fat Mother of God (which was not vulgar but, rather, complimentary in the hungry Middle Ages). Some names were only vaguely religious in that they used the number three and thereby evoked the Trinity. The number three was extremely popular: The Three Catfish, The Three Goddesses, The Three Pruning Knives, The Three Torches, The Three Panes (this was a bakery and not a glazier's), The Three Nun's Coifs, The Three Doves, The Three Fish, The Three Pigeons, etc. These were only a few of the names used on the Rue Mouffetard, for each store had as many as its changing ownership required. Today, with the return of the small boutique, interesting names are again becoming common.

On your right, a little farther up the hill is the Rue l'Arbalète leading to the **Place des Patriarches**. It was here that the Maison du Patriarche once stood. This estate occupied the land

Standard for Aux Trois Ceps, No. 80 Rue Mouffetard

between the Rues Daubenton, Mouffetard, l'Epée de Bois, and Gracieuses. The house was set back from the street and was approached from an alley placed where you are now. The first owner was Jean de Meulan, the Bishop of Paris who pardoned the mendicant priests. The property passed through several hands before Simon de Cramault, Archbishop of Rheims and Patriarch of Alexandria bought it. It was then that the estate received the name Maison du Patriarche. This gradually was changed to Maison des Patriarches, when fuzzy memories associated Simon de Cramault with the Patriarch of Jerusalem, Guillaume de Chanac, and it was assumed that they had lived on the same property.

The fate of Simon de Cramault is disputed by historians: Some say he was evicted from his house for not paying a tax to the Abbey Ste. Geneviève. Others say, more logically, that he was forced to abandon the house when Jean Sans Peur, Duke of Burgundy, pillaged the entire village on his way to Paris, followed by the Armagnacs who occupied it, and finally the English who devastated it. Whatever the reason, Cramault did not have enough money to run the estate and in 1443 abandoned it to Thibault Canaye, a hotel owner on Rue de la Harpe and husband of the wealthy Gobelins wool factory heiress, Mathurine Gobelin.

The house remained in this family until, in the sixteenth century, Jean Canaye, a great-great-grandson and militant Calvinist, rented it to a friend who opened the house to the Huguenots. The Huguenots turned the house into a Protestant temple, one of the two that had been allowed in the villages outside Paris. The Catholics of the Bourg St. Marcel were not at all pleased to see the Huguenots installed right beside their church, and on Saturday, December 27, 1561, the first religious violence in Paris broke out here. It was the holiday of St. John the Evangelist, and 2,000 Protestants had all gathered to hear Jean Malo, the old pastor of St. André des Arts, give a special sermon. The congregation was unable to hear the sermon, however, because the sexton of St. Médard insisted on repeatedly ringing the bells for vespers only 200 feet away. Malo sent four men to the church to ask the priest for quiet, but that was a serious mistake, for they fell into an ambush. When they arrived at the church doors, one man was snatched inside and beaten by parishioners. He was never seen alive again. The other three helplessly faced a locked-up church front, while stones and slate rained on them from above.

The three men returned to the Maison du Patriarche ready to draw blood. The Huguenots quickly armed themselves and stormed the church. They killed and wounded parishioners, broke all the religious statues and windows, profaned the altar, and sacked the sacristy, throwing holy wafers to the wind. The Catholics, in retaliation, burned the temple and then called for government support. Anne de Montmorency, head of the royal army, authorized the Catholics to raze one section of the house and to execute four of the Protestant offenders. The Catholics turned the execution into a public spectacle. Near the portals of St. Médard the prisoners had both hands cut off and their tongues pierced. Then they were gently strangled so as not to expire entirely and finally were burned to death. As a final measure the Catholics confiscated all their goods to pay for the repairs to the church. There were only six buildings, a garden, and some dependencies left to the estate when it passed into the hands of Maréchal Biron, who authorized the construction of the *marché* on the site of the house.

Up the street at **No. 12 Rue Mirbel** you will find an excellent restaurant, Vellu. Try the terrine or their chicken specialty.

Return to the Rue Mouffetard, to **No. 75,** and the restaurant Jardin de la Mouff, which boasts that you will be able to eat your dinner in the middle of Paris looking out into a quiet garden. They do have a glass wall in the back, but the garden outside is only a small patch of grass and one tree. The restaurant, though, is very pleasant and *intime*. They have an interesting menu offering two fixed price dinners at moderate rates. The food is standard French fare: boeuf bourguignon, coq au vin, artichokes in a vinaigrette sauce, and so on. For dessert the *tarte* Tatin, an upside-down apple tart, is excellent. See recipe, page 171.

Above the entrance to **No. 69** is a curious decoration in the form of a tree. The sign is carved from an old masthead taken from a sunken ship. There were two identical standards carved from the wood, and both advertised a restaurant named Au Vieux Chêne (at the old oak tree). The second once stood on the Right Bank, but the building there has been demolished. Wood from sunken ships is said to have a strange power, and mastheads that have been refashioned are supposedly even more potent. Legend has it that the two restaurants bearing these trees were cursed, particularly the one before you now. Every seven years, we're told, there was an unexpected argument at Au Vieux Chêne, and someone would die a violent death, right in front of the other diners. The first restaurant owner was forced to sell the property, because he could not cope with the macabre reputation attached to it. A second owner took over but also fell victim to the curse and eventually sold out to a discothèque owner who sold out to the present owner. (At the second Vieux Chêne strange, but not quite so violent, episodes allegedly occurred every 14 years.)

Across the street at **Nos. 76-74** is a neighborhood activities center in combination with two small experimental theaters. The center is open to all and offers courses in dance (modern and jazz), yoga, expressive movement, pottery, enameling, drama, and anything else they can find teachers for, for both adults and children. They also run a day-care center and train young people to start activity centers of their own. During the year the center organizes weekend trips for children to the country, and in summer they extend the trips to month-long visits, among them a special one in August to the seaside.

The center runs a constant deficit, particularly acute since the 1968 riots when it gave sanctuary to its young members who were fleeing the police. Ever since then the government has refused to give it any financial aid. In addition to perennial financial difficulties the center has demolition problems. You will have noted that the property consists of two buildings separated by a vacant lot. This is the result of interrupted renovations: The architect walked out in the middle of the job (he wanted to be paid), leaving the impecunious center with a gaping hole in its middle. Hence the "temporary" wooden buttressing that you see today. This support is examined by the city yearly and heavily taxed, and although the plans to rebuild are ready, no money is available.

The theaters attached to the center, **Théâtre de la Mouff** and the **Théâtre Troglodyte,** produce innovative plays by young playwrights. They use only professionals, some of them once students at the center. A few years ago the production of *Jesus Fric Super Crak* was written by one of the students. There are no performances on Sunday or Monday.

No. 64 is a true working-class shoestore. Here you can find real peasant *sabots,* wooden shoes that farmers and laborers wear to this day. They also sell woolen slipper *sabot* linings, rubber boots, and plain *espadrilles.* This store has no pretensions and no style; the goods are simply laid out on racks before you as in a bargain basement.

No. 62 is a beautifully restored seventeenth-century

building. Go in the apartment entrance and down the original stone hallway with the beamed ceiling. On your right is an excellent example of a Louis XIII staircase with its solid, rounded oak balustrades. The first diagonal section is a reproduction; the sections above are original. At the end of the hall is a small stone courtyard; to the left is a stone balcony with plants. Although we did not see the interior of any of these apartments, you can be sure that they have been skillfully redone and cost a great deal of money. It is just this sort of restoration that is changing the character of the Rue Mouffetard and many other streets of old Paris. Esthetically this is progress, but socially it means serious dislocation of the residents. These fine houses, on their medieval foundations, must be repaired and restored, but the high prices and rents that follow limit occupancy to the "nouveau chic." All over Paris the traditional residents of the various areas are being pushed out as the character of the streets, as well as the houses themselves, change.

Next door on the corner at **No. 60** is an unusual wall that masks a fountain built in 1624 (redone in 1671). The fountain exists because of Marie de Médicis. When Henry IV built the palace at the Luxembourg Gardens for her, she demanded a plumbing system that would be able to handle enough water for the palace and for the gardens. The only way to do this was to reopen and repair the ancient Gallo-Roman aqueduct. This brought so much water into the Left Bank, however, that 14 new fountains had to be built along the aqueduct's route to pump off the excess. This remaining fountain on the Rue Mouffetard is now a classified historical monument, which in this case seems to mean unattended. The explanatory plaque that was once carved into the stone has worn away into illegibility and finally disappeared, smothered by posters that creep higher and higher up the wall.

No. 61 was once a convent devoted to poor and sick women. The nuns of the Convent of Notre Dame de la Miséricorde bought this property, which stretched back to Rue Gracieuses, in 1653. By the beginning of the eighteenth century, however, the buildings were falling into ruins. In 1717 help came from an unexpected source. Madame de Maintenon, between her marriage to the poet Paul Scarron and her secret marriage to Louis XIV, had lived in a similar convent on the Rue des Minimes. She was always grateful for the hospitality she had

Entrance to No. 69, Rue Mouffetard

received, and so now, as an all-powerful marquise, she arranged for all the convent's expenses to come from the royal treasury. She ordered the lieutenant general of the police, Marc-René d'Argenson, to supervise the reconstruction. The convent's problems were not, however, at an end. D'Argenson did not have the morals a man in his position was expected to have, and when he came to supervise the work he had just separated from his latest mistress. During his brief inspection d'Argenson fell madly in love with a young and innocent novice; he tried to seduce her with promises of money. When the mother superior heard of the scheme, she took steps to make it impossible for the novice to leave. D'Argenson was furious and in retaliation informed her that he was suspending all construction until she gave in to his demands. The mother superior was thus forced to choose between the soul of her novice and the stones of her convent. The restoration took precedence, and the novice was yielded up to d'Argenson. (Whether she ever got the promised fortune is not known.)

No. 53. A buried treasure was found inside the walls of the building that once stood here. In 1938 No. 53 was condemned for reasons of safety by the city, and a crew of men were assigned to tear it down. On the first day of the job, a wrecker, Flammo Maures, ripped open a wall and was astounded to see "medals" pour forth. In no time all the workers gathered around and divided up the booty. When Maures went home that night, he showed his discovery to his wife, who immediately recognized the medals as gold. A law-abiding citizen, Maures took his "medals" to the police, where they were identified as Louis d'or old gold pieces. The treasure was reassembled, and the walls carefully searched, finally yielding a collection of 3,351 20-carat gold coins, in the form of double Louis weighing 16.3 grams each, single Louis weighing 8.7 grams, and half Louis weighing 4.7 grams. With the gold, an identifying piece of paper was also found: *"moi, sieur Louis Nivelle, écuyer et secrétaire du Roy, Legue ma fortune à ma fille, Anne-Louise Nivelle"* (I, Sir Louis Nivelle, assistant and secretary of the King, bequeath my fortune to my daughter, Anne-Louise Nivelle). The paper was not dated, but it was not difficult to uncover that Nivelle had been the secretary of Louis XV and had played a main role in a still unclarified mystery, vanishing in 1757 without leaving a trace.

The police, searching for the descendants of Anne-Louise, finally found General Robert de St. Vincent, who, although surprised, said that he had been brought up with a family tradition of a lost inheritance. It was not until 1952 that a legal division of the gold was arranged. Two hundred and fifty-four pieces had to be sold to pay the genealogists for their research, 538 were given to the city officials, and the original wrecking crew and the 84 descendants of Anne-Louise Nivelle split the remaining 2,559 coins. The gold was valued at 160,000 francs, $32,000 at that time, simply as metal; its historical value is untold.

Visit **Eugénie Phung** at No. 52. She makes new creations from old pieces of embroidered material at old-fashioned prices.

No. 36 was the shop of an old junk dealer. Today a young woman runs one of the few spruced-up antique (late nineteenth- and early twentieth-century) stores on the street. Her shop was filled with buyers; other shops are sure to come. The courtyard of No. 36 is worth a look; it is like suddenly being in a farmyard rather than the city. The buildings were once a secondary school (called a *collège*) and then housed a garrison of the Garde Française in the eighteenth century. Today the young come here for karate lessons. Look up into the large apartment on the second floor, on your left, to see the fine beams and staircases that are, for the most part in this building, still hidden under its poor exterior. On the right is an old well, still in use; at the back is another large doorway leading to a second courtyard and a narrow alley to the Rue Tournefort. Go through and look if you can. The last time we went the concierge was shocked and upset that we had found the door unlocked and were therefore able to walk through just as we had many times before.

Nos. 34, 26, 24, and 22. These are four more examples of attractively restored buildings. No. 34 has an iron-grill door opening to a long hall that leads to the semirestored building behind. Notice the original well in the left-hand stone wall of this hallway.

Above the door at **No. 12** is a recent wall decoration most Americans find astounding. The name of the building is Le Nègre Joyeux, the happy Negro, and the painting depicts a young black servant waiting on his mistress. America has long since rejected and condemned the image of the "happy black servant," but up till now in Europe no objections seem to have been raised against this stereotype.

PLACE CONTRESCARPE

To your right the street widens out to form the Place Contrescarpe. Take a seat in the center and look around. **Warning**—we found these cafés rude and expensive. This square has been described as the most picturesque in Paris, and although we would not go as far as that, the *place* is certainly one of the most interesting ones, especially on a summer night. Contrescarpe is a hangout and has been one for hundreds of years. The name goes back to the Middle Ages, when the Porte Bourdelles, one of the gates in Phillip Augustus's wall around Paris, stood just beyond this point on what is now the Rue Descartes. Outside the gate and its guard towers was the moat, rising to another earthen wall or counterescarpment (*contrescarpe*). At this time the Bourg St. Marcel was not really populated above what is now the Rue l'Epée de Bois, and so the land outside the gates became a no-man's-land. It gradually developed into a meeting spot where people naturally congregated, although no one lived there. During this early period in the fourteenth century, there were only three streetlights in Paris, none of them here, making the Place Contrescarpe a dark and dangerous area at night. Throughout the sixteenth century hopeless ordinances were passed (in 1504, 1526, and 1551), ordering each house in Paris to burn a candle in the first-floor window from 9 to 12 every night. Whether this was ignored or whether the candles were ineffectual, the police estimated an average of 15 bodies every morning from the killings of the night before—a fantastic homicide rate for what was by today's standards a small town.

In 1662 a priest, l'abbé Caraffe, invented mobile lighting. Place Contrescarpe soon picked up this innovation, and lamp carriers, or *lampadophores*, would wait here for customers. The lamp bearer would offer to accompany you right to your door, whether it was on the first or seventh floor, for five sous a slice of wax on his torch, or three sous for one-quarter hour with an oil lantern. In the eighteenth century this practice spread to umbrella carriers, who would protect you from showers on a time basis, and chair carriers to keep you out of the mud. At the turn of the eighteenth century lanterns attached to house fronts with a rope pulley were tried, but the candles blew out and the glass darkened. Besides, the city chose to save money by not using the lighting on moonlit nights or in the summers. It was not until the 1770s that any kind of effective street lighting was instituted, and the *lampadophores* were put out of business.

The actual *place* as it stands today was not created until 1852. By this time the area had the taverns and action that made it a logical site for a barracks of the Garde Républicaine. Today the Garde Républicaine is mostly decorative; the ruffians who used to inhabit the area have been replaced by winos, or *clochards*, who have long staked their claim here. For them this area offers every convenience: The Rue Mouffetard has the wine stores; the *marché* throws out spoiled food twice daily; the students and tourists are good marks for begging (a cigarette, if not money); and the Place Contrescarpe and the Rue Lacépède offer subway heating vents to sleep on. On almost any night you will see the *clochards* huddled on the vents in groups of three or four. They are bundled in rags and coated with a layer of protective dirt. When a rehabilitation center tried to help by taking the *clochards* in off the winter streets and giving them food and showers before returning them to the city, the center discovered to its shock that some of the clochards could no longer survive without their layer of dirt and died of the cold. The misery of their condition seems in a strange way to keep them going. They show little interest in a good meal and a bed; they have the opportunity to go to a hospice in Nanterre by free bus every night and be returned to the city the next day, but as one wino explained to us, no self-respecting, true *clochard* would consider this, except in time of dire need. In fact, they carefully cultivate their deterioration for the sake of their begging. A café-owner friend of ours told us how one day a *clochard* came in begging a free drink. Our friend, rather than give him a drink, asked the wino how someone so young could get into such a position. The *clochard* was visibly upset that she could tell he was still a young man. He had grown his beard and hair and not washed for days in order to look older and more pitiful, but his eyes had given him away as a still unseasoned bum.

The *clochards* are harmless and are nothing to be afraid of. They will call out for change or a cigarette from their prostrate positions as you pass, but you have no reason to be afraid to refuse them or to comply, whichever you prefer.

The French are generally disapproving of these outcasts and have little understanding or patience for them. Compared to some of the contemptuous comments in guidebooks of the Victorian era, however, some progress in social attitude has been made. Here is perhaps the prize comment we found made by an Englishman, F. Berkley Smith, in a book called *The Real Latin Quarter*, written in 1901, "That women should become outcasts through the hopelessness of their position or the breaking down of their brains can be understood, but that men of ability should sink into the dregs and stay there seems incredible. But it is often so."

In the 1950s the *clochards* of the Place Contrescarpe began having to share their territory with students and beatniks. Now the takeover is almost complete, and French and foreign hippies dominate the night scene. The restaurants and cafés put their tables out on the sidewalks, the food is cheap, and conversation is easy. Sometimes on the weekend a fire- and sword-swallower will come to entertain. These performers talk interminably, passing the hat all the while, and when the crowd is about to leave in disgust, they quickly prepare their act. At that point the police invariably appear to break up the crowd and chase or arrest the performers. The last time we saw these actors, one man, safety pin through his left nipple and covered with tattoos, was entirely wrapped in a chain that he was preparing to break out of, Houdini-style, when the police arrived. The crowd rapidly dispersed, and the chained man's partner disappeared, leaving him to face the music alone. In his agitation he couldn't make his Houdini trick work, and he was forced to stand there helplessly in his own bindings while the police questioned him. They let him off with a warning. As the police drove off, his partner miraculously reappeared.

The building at **No. 1** Place Contrescarpe has La Pomme de Pin (the pine cone) carved into its wall, referring to an old café that once stood on the square. The café was not in that building, however, which is modern, but in what is now a *charcuterie* on the corner of the Rue Blainville, to your left as you face La Pomme de Pin. It was here that the Pléiade Society came into being. This was a literary group begun in 1549 by Pierre Ronsard, Joachim du Bellay, and Jean Baïf. These young men had all come to Paris for their education and were engaged in studying the classics, which they did avidly, straight through the night. From their interest in classical poetry they felt a great need "to defend the French language and render it illustrious." Their purpose was to create a poetic language that would renew the art of versification and to invent the rhythms and the forms for French that would be the most harmonious and varied. The society had a strong influence on the French language, and their stylistic theories are still in use today.

RUE BLAINVILLE

Walk two blocks down the Rue Blainville to **No. 9,** which was the first public library in Paris. When we came to visit this beautiful eighteenth-century building with its large green courtyard we were met at the door by two policemen. When we asked what the problem was, they explained that since the building next door had been demolished, the left wing of this house was threatening to collapse. When we wondered what they would be able to do when the building did collapse, they said gaily, "Oh! We'll save people." Let's hope that by the time you visit, you won't have to be rescued *in extremis.*

During the revolution, **No. 11,** the adjacent building, was occupied by a strange, mystical woman. Her given name was Catherine Théot, but she called herself the Mère de Dieu, Mother of God. She put herself forward as a prophetess with a mission to Robespierre. The hard-nosed Jacobin revolutionaries, however, were not at all impressed with her feats; in fact, they felt that she was unwittingly contributing to her hero's downfall through ridicule. In order to obtain evidence against the Mother of God, the police sent two men to pretend to join her cult. The ritual was recorded in the police records by one of the men. He reported that on 18 Floréal, an II (May 7, 1794), they went to the door, where they were met by a servant who led in the first policeman saying, "Come mortal man towards immortality. The Mother of God permits you to enter." They went in, and a disciple known as the illuminator, *éclaireuse,* rang a bell. Curtains parted, and two young girls helped the Mother of God to her chair. They kissed her slipper and chanted, "Glory to the Mother of God!" The mother then spoke to one of the policemen, "Do you want the light?"

"Yes," he answered.

"Can you read?"

"A little."

"I will admit you my son. Clasp your hands."

At this point the *éclaireuse* grasped his head while the Mother of God kissed him on the eyelids, the forehead, the left cheek, twice on the chin and behind his right ear. He returned the

kisses. The *éclaireuse* then announced, "Mother and son, kiss each other on the mouth!" He submitted stoically to this last requirement and was accepted. Once initiated, he had no trouble gathering the evidence of fraudulent deification (a strange crime in a regime that was busily manufacturing its own new Goddess of Reason) and soon the entire cult was in the net. The Mother of God, in her fury, swore she would never die on the scaffold. "An event that will shock all Paris will announce my death!" she declared. In fact, she died of natural causes at 78 on the fourteenth of Fructidor, an II (August 31, 1794), a prisoner in the Conciergerie. (Robespierre had himself been killed a few weeks before in the Coup of Thermidor.) As she died the powder stores at Grenelle exploded, killing hundreds and breaking all the windows in Paris. Her disciples were dispatched by the guillotine.

Return to Place Contrescarpe and continue up the Rue Mouffetard. The **Crêperie de la Mouffe** at No. 19 is a good way to manage a light meal in Paris. They offer almost 80 kinds of crêpes here, approximately 40 of buckwheat (*sarrasin*) with main-course-type fillings and an equal number of dessert crêpes made with wheat flour. The buckwheat crêpes include ham, cheese, salad, fried eggs, a tomato-onion mixture, sausages, and more, plus combinations of everything, for very cheap prices. The dessert crêpes, however, are the best part of the menu. People have been known to take half an hour to make this critical choice. The range goes from crêpes with plain melted chocolate to crêpes with bananas *flambées* (with cointreau or grand marnier) to crêpes with caramelized apples with fresh or whipped cream (*crème fraiche* or *crème chantilly*), to the summer specialty and our favorite, crêpes with fresh strawberries and cream. The quality of food here is generally good, except for an occasional dry and brittle crêpe; on the average, they are certainly far superior to the street-corner version. Our only objection to this restaurant is the slowness of the service, but drink your bowls of cider and relax. There is no other way. The atmosphere makes up for the wait; the place is young, friendly, and crowded, and the waitresses are always nice about the delays. The recipe for the crêpes on page 169 is from P.C., a friend of ours and the best Breton crêpe maker in the Old World or New.

At the intersection with the Rue Thouin, the Rue Mouffetard becomes the Rue Descartes. Where you are standing was the emplacement of the Porte Bourdelles and its guard towers; they were demolished in 1685. There are still remains of Phillip Augustus's wall, however, at **No. 47** Rue Descartes. Go into this historically classified building, and take the third staircase (a winding seventeenth-century one) up to the second door that leads outside. Suddenly it is as though you were on a secret street, above ground. You are actually standing on the top of the medieval wall. (The buildings along the old wall all made thrifty use of it as their fourth side. The curved building ahead of you on the right is that way simply because, when the original house was built, that was the contour of the wall at that point.) Back downstairs in the entrance hallway look closely at the stone slabs you are walking on. Two on the left have numbers carved into their faces. These are stones that were taken from the cemetery of Ste. Geneviève when it was destroyed in the eighteenth century. (Again, a little saving in construction costs.) The numbers probably refer to lists of the people buried in communal graves dating from the sixteenth and seventeenth century.

Across the street and to the right at **No. 38** is a tiny, triangular antique store put up by building one wall across the angle of the other two. The objects for sale here are mostly bric-a-brac. The girl who runs the store often has interesting antique children's toys and books, silver objects, china, and a little of everything unusual. Her hours are very irregular, however, so you're always taking a chance on finding her in. Even if the shop is closed and the deceptive sign implying imminent reopening is up (don't believe it), take a look in the windows. Everything is visible from the street, and you may find an incentive to wait.

At **No. 39** there is a plaque stating that the poet Verlaine died here in 1896.

From here you are within walking distance of the Arènes de Lutèce, the remains of a Roman arena on the Rue Monge; the Jardin des Plantes, the botanical gardens with a small zoo; and on the same street, Rue Geoffroy St. Hilaire, the Mosque, the only mosque in Paris. It also includes a charming Turkish café. In the other direction in the Place du Panthéon there is the Panthéon, a burial place of famous French men, and the Church of Ste. Geneviève, with its unusual architecture and famous wood screen.

A NOTE TO PARISWALKERS

Now that you have walked and looked and made some of Paris yours, we hope you will be able to continue on your own—in Paris and other cities as well. Because citywalking is a technique that is applicable everywhere, it will work in London, Rome, New York . . .

Recipes

These recipes were not chosen with any balance in mind. They are a combination of our requests and what the chefs were willing to give. They represent the typical experience of anyone who enjoys the traditional dishes and their variations, as well as examples of foreign food, an important aspect of the French restaurant scene today. We have tried all these recipes, some of them several times. They work.

We have included:

Omelette Brayaude (cream and potato omelet) from Auberge des Deux Signes

Coquilles St. Jacques en Brochette (scallops on a skewer) from Atelier Maître Albert

Veau Matelote (veal in red wine sauce) from Chez Allard

Bric (lamb and veal in pastry) from Au Vieux Paris

Tournedos Bûcherie (beef fillet on apples with mushroom sauce) from La Bûcherie

Crêpes Bretonnes (Breton pancakes) from Pierrette Coadou

Tarte Tatin (upside-down apple tart) from Jardin de la Mouff

Flambiche (pudding with fruit) from Auberge des Deux Signes

OMELETTE BRAYAUDE

This cream and potato omelet is served as an hors d'oeuvre or as a lunch dish at the Auberge des Deux Signes. Brayaude is a region in Auvergne, the central plateau of France.

INGREDIENTS: *serves 2*

2 medium potatoes
¼ lb. salt pork, bacon, or beef bacon substitute
4 eggs
2 oz. sour cream
¾ oz. blond Wisconsin cheddar, grated
¼ tsp. salt and a pinch of pepper
1 tsp. vegetable shortening
chopped parsley

PREPARATION

1. Cut the salt pork, which should have meat running through it, into ½-inch cubes, and melt them over low heat with a tsp. of shortening. If bacon or substitute is used, blanch it for 10 minutes in boiling water to remove the smoky taste. The cubes should not be completely melted, however; some small bits should remain in the pan.

2. Peel, wash, and dry the potatoes. Cut them into ¼-inch cubes and brown them slowly in the melted fat.

3. While the potatoes are cooking, beat the eggs with the salt and pepper.

4. In another bowl mix the cheese and sour cream, and set the mixture aside.

5. When the potatoes are brown, pour the eggs over them. As the eggs begin to firm up, gently break the cooked surface in a few places to expose more of the liquid to the heat of the pan.

ASSEMBLING

1. When the omelet is practically finished, spoon the cream mixture across the center.

2. Then as you slide the omelet onto the serving dish, fold it over, decorate with chopped parsley, and serve. If you wish to make this for more than two people, keep the first one in the oven while you make the next. Four eggs is the most that can be conveniently handled at once.

COQUILLES ST. JACQUES EN BROCHETTE

Even when the French turn to barbecuing scallops on a skewer, they use a fine sauce. Here is an easy way, from the Atelier Maître Albert, to make the white butter sauce for fish, *beurre blanc,* to nap on the scallops.

INGREDIENTS: *6-8 skewers*

SKEWER
24 large scallops
3 large green peppers
12 small onions or pieces of onion
6 lemons

SAUCE
½ cup white wine vinegar
1 tbs. shallots or scallions, finely chopped
salt and pepper to taste
2 egg yolks
12 oz. butter (3 sticks)

PREPARATION

1. Thread a skewer in the following order: half a lemon, scallop, green pepper, and onion. Repeat the last three items three or four times, depending on the length of the skewer, and end with another half lemon.

2. Boil vinegar, shallots, salt, and pepper, until they are reduced to a moist mixture, about a tablespoon full.

3. Remove from fire and add egg yolks to the onion mixture. Then add the melted butter. Whip over the lowest heat possible until sauce is thick. This is a simple way to prepare white butter sauce.

ASSEMBLING

1. Place the skewers on aluminum foil, nap with the sauce, and place under broiler. If you are barbecuing, simply lay the skewers on the grill.

2. Cook very quickly, just until color begins to appear. The less you cook the scallop the better.

3. Be sure to keep the remaining sauce warm in a bowl near the pilot light or near a low burner until ready to serve. Too much heat makes the sauce oily.

VEAU MATELOTE

Allard, a long-time famous gourmet restaurant with no pretensions (the cooks work in the open right opposite the front door) is well known for this rich, red-wine, veal dish. *Matelot* is the familiar French word for sailor. The *matelote* is the sailor's wife. The word comes from the Dutch, *mattenoot,* no doubt related to the English mate. Sailors love red wine, and it is not surprising that the sailor's wife would very naturally use it and some onions to prepare the fish her husband brought home. The gourmet, of course, uses white wine for fish and also for veal. Hence, the word *matelote* is used to describe a dish of fish or veal made with red wine and onions.

INGREDIENTS: *serves 8-9*

enough oil to saute ingredients
4 lb. veal stew meat or veal shoulder
¾ lb. salt pork or bacon
3 medium white onions
¾ cup brandy
1½ bottles red burgundy wine
1½ tbs. tomato paste
2 tsp. salt
1 tsp. pepper
1 tsp. sugar
bouquet garni—bay leaf, thyme, parsley tied with a string
2 cloves garlic, crushed
1½ cups chicken bouillon

PREPARATION

1. Cut the veal into pieces about three times bite size; it will shrink about one third. If the meat has any tough outer skin, remove it.

2. Blanch the salt pork fat or bacon to remove the salty or smoky taste. If you use bacon, cut it into 1-inch pieces, large enough to be visible in the final dish. It loses half its size in the cooking. If you use the salt pork fat cut it like a bacon slice but ½ inch thick, make sure meat is included in each slice, then cube it.

3. Dice the onions.

COOKING

1. Use an enameled or iron casserole, the bottom of which measures at least 8 or 10 inches. Heat 2 tbs. of oil and add one third of the meat. Sprinkle 1 tbs. flour on the veal and keep turning the veal as it browns. Transfer the veal to a large bowl or pan. Continue this process until all the meat is browned. Add oil as required. Next saute the bacon, and transfer to the bowl with the veal. Then saute the onions until translucent. Return the meat and bacon to the casserole with the

onions. Heat to a boil and sprinkle the ¾ cup of brandy on top. Light with a match and wait for the flame to burn out by itself. Turn the heat off while you make the wine sauce.

2. Put the wine, bouquet garni, garlic, tomato paste, salt, pepper, and sugar in a large saucepan. Let it come to a boil, then light it with a match and let the flame burn out. Next add 1½ cups of chicken bouillon.

3. Pour this sauce over the meat, and simmer the entire mixture for 40 minutes. Make sure nothing sticks to the bottom of the casserole. Lower heat if necessary.

4. Now transfer the meat with a large slotted spoon to a bowl. Discard the bouquet garni, and reduce the sauce to one half its volume. The sauce should boil until it slides slowly off the back of a wooden spoon and has a velvety consistency. This should take about one hour.

5. Return the veal to the reduced sauce. Remove the excess fat (perhaps ½ cup) with a baster before heating and serving. Serve with parsleyed potatoes. If you think your guests won't soak up the sauce with their bread, however, serve the dish with rice instead. Goes well with burgundy wine. Veau Matelote tastes even better the next day.

BRIC

M. Nico at Au Vieux Paris and his father before him have been making this Greek dish for the past 35 years. This combination of veal and lamb with an egg on top is wrapped in thin golden crusts.

INGREDIENTS: *serves 6*

1 lb. lamb from the leg of lamb
1 lb. veal from the forequarter or shin, stew meat
1 large onion, chopped
2 tbs. coarse salt
¼ tsp. white pepper
1 tsp. oregano
1 tsp. thyme
Package of phyllo pastry leaves
6 eggs
1 cup oil
1 egg white

PREPARATION

1. Cut or chop lamb and veal into small bits. Do not grind.
2. Mix meat with onions and seasonings.
3. Place in an 8-inch pyrex dish and bake in 350° oven for 1¼ hours.

ASSEMBLING

1. Cut three layers of phyllo leaves into a 6-inch square. Place 3-4 tbs. of cooked meat in the center of leaves.
2. Brush edges with egg white.
3. Break an egg on top of the meat.
4. Bring all the edges of the pastry up over the center of the meat and brush with more egg white to hold it in place. M. Nico folds his pastry into a triangle. We couldn't manage that but found our way very easy.

COOKING

1. Put 1 cup of oil in a frying pan.
2. When the oil is hot, place the folded pastry in the oil. Sprinkle the top side with some of the oil; it keeps it puffy.
3. The pastry will turn golden very quickly; turn it to the other side for a minute or until crisp and golden.
4. The bric may be kept warm in the oven if not served immediately or while you prepare more of them. The bric may also be baked in a 350° oven for 20 minutes until golden and puffed, if you wish to avoid frying.

TOURNEDOS BUCHERIE

A tournedos is a filet mignon traditionally served on toast and smothered with sauce. Escoffier, the great turn-of-the-century chef, knew how to spread the fame of his dishes by naming them after the celebrated artists of the day: toast and peaches after the coloratura Nellie Melba, tournedos after Rossini. Escoffier's tournedos consisted of truffles and foie gras on a fillet napped in Madeira and veal sauce. The style took hold and variations on the tournedos became the vogue. M. Bosque, at the Bûcherie has a particularly different and delicious arrangement. Crust and apples and foie gras and creamy mushroom sauce surround this tender cut of meat.

INGREDIENTS: *serves 6*

APPLE TART
2 cups flour
⅛ tsp. baking powder
7 tbs. shortening or 5 tsp. butter and 2 tbs. shortening
1 egg beaten with 1-2 tbs. water
3 apples, Golden Delicious

MUSHROOMS
1 lb. mushrooms
juice of 1 lemon
2 tbs. butter
salt and pepper

BECHAMEL SAUCE
4 tbs. butter
4 tbs. flour
8 oz. milk
8 oz. light cream

TOURNEDOS
6 fillets of beef
3 oz. port
4 oz. chicken bouillon
1 tbs. tomato puree
6 slices of foie gras

PREPARATION FOR THE APPLE TART

Mix the flour and baking powder. Cut the butter into the flour and blend with your fingers until the mixture is the size of peas.
2. Add the egg, beaten with cold water, and knead the mixture together.
3. Gather the dough into a ball and refrigerate at least one hour.

4. Divide the dough into six equal parts and roll each one out on a floured board. Cut circles to fit individual tart molds. If you have no mold, simply cut a circle the size of your fist, about 4 inches. Core and peel apples, and place thin slices of half an apple on each crust.

5. Bake in 350° oven on a cookie sheet for about 10 minutes or until pastry is golden. These can be reheated before serving, if necessary. Frozen patty shells may be used if you prefer.

PREPARATION FOR THE MUSHROOMS

1. Wash and cut the mushrooms into small chunks. Add them to 2 tbs. of hot butter in the frying pan.

2. Add the juice of one lemon, salt, and pepper.

3. Simmer for 5 minutes.

PREPARATION FOR THE BECHAMEL SAUCE

1. Heat 4 oz. of butter until bubbly.

2. Add 4 tbs. of flour all at once, and stir this with a wooden spoon until there are no lumps.

3. Add (slowly at first) 1 cup of milk and 1 cup of cream (or 2 cups of milk, if you wish.)

4. Stir until the sauce is almost thick enough to hold its shape.

5. Add the strained mushrooms to the cream sauce.

PREPARATION FOR THE TOURNEDOS

1. Heat a heavy skillet with 1 tbs. of oil and 1 tbs. of butter.

2. When this bubbles add the tournedos. Let them cook for 3 to 4 minutes on each side and remove. The meat should be crusty on the outside and very red on the inside. Add 4 oz. of port to the skillet and bring to a boil. Then add the 4 tbs. chicken bouillon, mixed with 1 tbs. of tomato puree to the port and swirl around for a few minutes to reduce and slightly thicken it.

ASSEMBLING

Place the tournedos on the apple tart, cap the meat with a slice of foie gras, then top it with ½ cup of mushroom sauce. Finally, pour a thin ring of the port mixture on the cream sauce and serve.

CREPES BRETONNES

A crêpe is thin; a pancake is thick. You smother a pancake; you stuff a crêpe. This is a dessert recipe from Pierrette Coadou. In order to use it with food (chicken, cheese, etc.), simply omit the sugar.

INGREDIENTS: *50 crêpes*

2 cups sifted flour
½ tsp. salt
1 cup sugar
1/3 cup water
4 large eggs or 5 small ones
2 cups milk
1 tbs. oil
1 stick of butter

PREPARATION

1. The batter is not difficult to mix by hand. Mix flour, sugar, and salt in a bowl.
2. Add water in thirds, mixing each time. Continue with the milk, until the mixture is smooth and shiny.
3. Then add the eggs, one at a time, and mix.
4. Add the rest of the milk and 1 tbs. of oil and mix. (To use a blender, add the milk, water, oil, eggs, sugar, salt, and then the flour. Blend for 1 minute. Scrape flour from the sides if necessary and blend it into the mixture.)
5. Let the batter rest overnight or at least for a few hours. Otherwise, it becomes elastic.

COOKING

1. Heat a 7-inch crêpe pan or American skillet on low heat. Peel back the paper from the end of a stick of cold butter and run it around the pan until the pan is covered with a thin layer.
2. When the butter begins to bubble and turns slightly brown, you are ready to add the batter. Use a ladle or measuring cup and pour 3 tbs. or 1½ oz. into the center of the pan. Lift the pan and swirl it around so that the batter covers the entire surface. Patch a hole, if necessary, with a drop of batter.
3. Just before turning the crêpe, dot the surface with the stick of butter. In less than a minute, when the underside is spotty brown, place a metal spatula under one third of the crêpe and turn it over. The second side is done in half the time. Your first crêpe might be a loss, the second will be fine.
4. Rub butter on the pan between making each crêpe. Do not leave the pan on the heat between crêpes unless you move quickly. Keep the crêpes warm by placing them on a plate over a pot with simmering water in it. They pile easily.

ASSEMBLING

1. The purists eat a crêpe plain. Fold it in half and half again and pick the triangle up in your hands and eat.

2. You may spread a crêpe with jam and/or whipped cream. Roll it into a cylinder, but don't eat it with your hands.

3. Crêpes may be stored in the freezer. Contrary to heated discussion, reheated crêpes taste very good.

LA TARTE DES DESMOISELLES TATIN

The Misses Tatin, who kept an inn at Lamotte-Beuvron, south of Orléans, were the inventors of this upside-down caramel apple tart. Since their day it has become famous all over France. M. Duval at the Jardin de la Mouff kindly gave us his recipe for an excellent version of the pie.

INGREDIENTS: *serves 8*

CRUST
1½ cups flour
2 tbs. sugar
¼ tsp. salt
4 oz. cold butter
5 tbs. cold water

APPLES
8 apples—Golden Delicious
4 oz. butter
2/3 cup sugar

PREPARATION FOR CRUST

1. Mix the flour, sugar, and salt.
2. Add the cold butter and cut it into the flour. To do this use two knives and draw them repeatedly against each other, through the butter, until the mixture is in small bits the size of peas.
3. Add the cold water, gathering the dough into a mass.
4. Knead the dough into a ball and refrigerate for at least an hour.

PREPARATION FOR APPLES

1. Peel and quarter the apples. Remove the core and slice each quarter into 4 slices.
2. Melt the butter in a large frying pan, add sugar, and mix.
3. Over high heat lay the apple slices on the bottom of the pan. Move the apples around to keep them from sticking and to allow them to color evenly. Turn the apples so that both sides will cook. When the apples and caramel are a golden, light-brown remove them from the stove. Be very careful with caramel; if it burns it will be black and bitter. Slide the apples and caramel into a well greased 10-inch pie dish. (The restaurant does it somewhat differently. Take a copper pie dish, and make the caramel in it. Stand the apples in the caramel in circles until the dish is filled. Cap the top with the rest of the apples, heat for 10 minutes before placing the crust on top.)

ASSEMBLING

1. Roll out the dough to ⅛-inch thickness, and cut a circle one inch more than the top of your pie dish.
2. Lay the crust over the apples and press the crust down on edge of the pan.

3. Pierce holes in the top of the crust, and bake in 350° oven until crust is well done, about 40 minutes.

4. Remove from oven and loosen edges. Place serving dish over pie dish and invert. Rearrange apples if necessary to make a smooth top.

5. This should be served warm (reheat in the oven for a few minutes) and with whipped cream.

FLAMBICHE

When a poor family could afford dessert, or a richer one wanted to use the leftover fruit, they made a flan. A flan consists of a thick crêpe batter with fruit of almost any kind—usually apple, cherry or pear—placed in it and baked in the oven. It is half cake, half pudding. The dish should be served warm; the English pour cream over it. The word "flan" means a round cake (**you** may make it in any shape pan) and comes from its similarity in shape to a blank metal disc, a *flan,* which was often used for stamping coins. This recipe comes from the Auberge des Deux Signes.

INGREDIENTS
BATTER
2¾ cup flour
5 whole eggs
1 tsp. oil
2¾ cup milk
1 tsp. baking powder
7 oz. butter
FRUIT
8 medium apples or pears, or 3 cups of fresh or canned cherries
¾ cup sugar

PREPARATION

1. Blend the eggs, oil, salt, milk, and the flour and baking powder in a blender until smooth and thick enough to coat the back of a wooden spoon. (For the hand method, see the crêpe recipe, p. 169.)
2. Cover the bowl with a cloth and let the batter rise in a warm place for at least an hour.
3. Then add the melted butter and mix.
4. Peel and core the apples, cut them in half vertically, then place the cut edge down on a board and cut semicircular wedges ¼-inch thick.
5. Sprinkle sugar on the apples and mix carefully until the surface of the apples is coated.

ASSEMBLING

1. Pour the batter into a buttered pyrex or baking dish that will later be served at the table. You may mix the apple slices into the batter or place them close together.
2. Place apples close together in rows **into** the batter. The apples should be at a 45° angle to the bottom of the dish with the round edge up. When the flan is finished these edges of the apples should be dark brown. Place pears in a similar pattern; cherries, one next to the other.
3. Bake one hour in 300° oven or until knife comes out clean.

Hotels and Restaurants

We have listed the hotels in three categories, but since luxury resides on the Right Bank, this list is primarily moderately priced, followed by student arrangements, which cost less than a few dollars a night.

L'HOTEL
13 Rue Des Beaux Arts, 6e, tel. 633-89-20 (near St. Germain des Prés). In this extraordinary hotel prices range from $50-$130. Most rooms on the street cost about $60.

HOTEL LE COLBERT
7 Rue de l'Hôtel Colbert, 5e, tel. 633-85-50 (near St. Julien le Pauvre). In this first-class hotel a double room costs $40, some singles for $35. See page 48.

The moderately priced hotels below charge about $20-$30 for a double room with bath, only slightly less for a single, about a third less without bath. The hotels are listed, within each area, in descending order of price, though the differences are small and often overlap. The very last ones are still good ones.

Area near St. Germain des Prés

MADISON HOTEL
143 Blvd. St. Germain, tel. 326-57-12. Opposite St. Germain.

SCANDINAVIA
27 Rue de Tournon, tel. Med. 45-20, métro Odéon. All doubles with bath, fine decoration, breakfast extra.

HOTEL DE NICE ET DES BEAUX-ARTS
4 Bis Rue des Beaux Arts, tel. 326-54-05. Quiet street near St. Germain des Prés.

HOTEL DU PAS DE CALAIS
59 Rue des Sts. Pères, tel. 548-78-74. Seventeenth-century building with modern furnishings.

HOTEL D'ANGLETERRE
44 Rue Jacob, tel. 548-87-91. Breakfast served in quiet, grassy courtyard.

HOTEL DES STS. PERES
65 Rue des Sts. Pères, tel. 548-44-45. Modern, breakfast in pleasant courtyard. Street of antiques.

HOTEL D'ISLY
29 Rue Jacob, tel. 326-64-41. Modern and quiet.

HOTEL DANUBE
58 Rue Jacob, tel. 548-42-70. Special arrangements for three or four in a room.

DEUX-CONTINENTS
25 Rue Jacob, tel. Dan. 72-46. Two buildings connected by stairways and courtyards. Modern, good lighting.

HOTEL DES MARRONIERS
21 Rue Jacob, tel. 033-91-66. Quiet, rooms facing garden particularly attractive.

Area near Huchette and St. Julien le Pauvre

HOTEL L'ALBE
1 Rue de la Harpe, tel. 033-14-45. Within sight of the Blvd. St. Michel and the river, in the heart of Left Bank activity.

GRAND HOTEL DU MONT-BLANC
28 Rue de la Huchette, tel. 033-49-44. Ask for quiet room on the courtyard on this crowded and fascinating street. See page 59.

HOTEL CLAUDE BERNARD
43 Rue des Ecoles, tel 326-32-52. English spoken, near the Blvd. St. Michel.

Hostels

FOYER BONAPARTE
24 Rue Bonaparte, 6e, tel. Dan. 65-45. July 1-September 30. Women only.

FOYER JANE VIALLE
14 Rue Rollin, 5e, tel. 033-10-11. June 1-October 1. Near Mouffetard.

The following is a selected list of restaurants in and near the areas of the walks. We have divided them into three categories in order of price and elegance, and given stars according to Michelin. These are the ones we know, but there are many others we have never tried that will become your great eating discoveries. Food in France is still the best.

Area near St. Julien le Pauvre

Extraordinary:

***LE TOUR D'ARGENT
15 Quai Tournelle, tel. 033-23-32. Supreme food and elegance with a view from above of the islands in the Seine below.

Excellent:

L'ATELIER DE MAITRE ALBERT
1 Rue Maître Albert, tel. 633-13-78. See pages 53-54; recipe, page 163.

L'AUBERGE DES DEUX SIGNES
46 Rue Galande, tel. 325-46-56. See the description of our favorite restaurant, pages 44-46; recipes, pages 162 and 173.

LA BUCHERIE
41 Rue de la Bûcherie, tel. 033-39-24. See pages 22-23; recipe, page 167. Open from 11 a.m. to 2 a.m.

*CHEZ MARIUS
30 Rue Fosses-St. Bernard, tel. 033-19-01. Bouillabaisse and lobster specialties.

LE MONGOL
12 Rue Frédéric Sauton, tel. 325-45-45. Combination Chinese and Japanese. Very fresh food prepared instantly before you.

AU PACTOLE
44 Blvd. St. Germain, tel. 326-92-28. Amazing meal for the price. Reserve ahead.

RAFFATIN ET HONORINE
16 Blvd. St. Germain, tel. 033-22-21. Stupendous hors d'oeuvres and wide choice of desserts make an entire meal.

SATAY
10 Rue St. Julien le Pauvre, tel. 033-31-33. See page 26.

Budget, but good:

A LA COQUILLE ST-JACQUES
79 Rue Galande. See page 39.

ASIA
57 Rue Galande, tel. 033-06-99. Modest, but interesting Creole specialties cooked in plain view. Orders can be taken out.

Area near La Huchette and St. Michel

Extraordinary:

*ALLARD
41 Rue St. André des Arts, tel. 326-48-23. See pages 86-87; recipe, page 164. Reserve well in advance.

ROTISSERIE PERIGOURDINE
2 Place St. Michel, tel. 326-70-54. Elegant, second floor overlooking the Seine.

Budget, but good:

ALSACIENNE
54 Blvd. St. Michel, tel. 326-53-31. Food store and restaurant. Sit outside in summer and watch the people go by.

LES BALKANS
3 Rue de la Harpe, tel. 326-20-96. Kebabs, goulash, and couscous for very little money on a lively street.

FLEUVE D' ARGENT
25 Rue St. André des Arts. Another tiny, inexpensive, Vietnamese restaurant run by a whole family.

ROTISSERIE ST. SEVERIN
6 Rue St. Séverin. See page 68. A handsome, but modest restaurant.

Area near St. Germain

Extraordinary:

*LAPEROUSE
51 Quai Grands-Augustins, tel. 326-68-04. Dining room and private rooms in this eighteenth-century mansion. Pillowy souffles of all sorts are the favorite dessert.

*RELAIS LOUIS XIII
8 Rue Grands-Augustins, tel. 326-75-96, métro Odéon. Authentic seventeenth-century decoration on an historic spot. Small but select menu, excellent *cave.*

MEDITERRANEE
2 Place Odéon, tel. 326-46-75, métro Odéon. Across from the Theater of France, menu designed by Jean Cocteau. Marseilles-type fish specialties.

Excellent:

BRASSERIE LIPP
151 Blvd. St. Germain, tel. 548-53-91. See p. 123

L'HOTEL
13 Rue des Beaux-Arts, tel. 633-89-20. See page 114. Lunch at a moderate price in a pretty garden patio.

MAITRE PAUL
Rue Monsieur le Prince, tel. 033-74-59, métro Odéon. Good solid food, lots of flowers. Reserve.

ROTISSERIE DE L' ABBAYE
22 Rue Jacob, tel. 326-36-26. Medieval costumes, singing troubadours, fine food, opens at 9 p.m.

Budget, but good:

AU VIEUX PARIS
2 Rue de l'Abbaye, 326-21-92. See page 101; recipe, page 166.

BEAUX-ARTS
11 Rue Bonaparte, tel. 326-92-64. Bistro filled with students from the art school across the street.

VAGENENDE
142 Blvd. St. Germain, tel. 326-68-18. Best buy. See page 124.

PETIT ZINC
25 Rue de Buci, tel. 033-79-34. Good bistro, open until 3 a.m.
In the heart of a busy market street.

PROCOPE
13 Rue l'Ancienne Comédie, tel. 326-99-20. Oldest restaurant
in Paris, richly reminiscent of such former guests as Robespierre, Ben Franklin, Balzac.

Area near Mouffetard

Excellent:

COUPE-CHOU
9 Rue de Lanneau, tel. 633-68-69, métro Maubert. Lots of
rooms, lots of fun, hearty food, decorated by the three actors
who run the restaurant.

LA TRUFFIERE
4 Rue Blainville, tel. 633-29-82. Specialists who bring out the
flavor of food with truffles. Last serving at midnight.

Budget, but good:

FELIX
23 Rue Mouffetard, tel. 707-68-78. Serves very late. Lively.

JARDIN DE LA MOUFF
75 Rue Mouffetard, tel. 707-19-29. See page 146; recipe, page
171.

LUU DINH
6 Rue Thouin, tel. 326-91-01. Vietnamese food served almost
entirely by the boss.

LA MONTAGNE PELEE
13 Rue Tournefort, tel. 707-01-39. Antilles food. Serves late.
Three guitarists.

LE MOUFF
5 Rue Mouffetard, tel. 033-97-33. For under twenty-fives.

LE REQUIN CHAGRIN
Place de la Contrescarpe, tel. 033-18-87. In the center of
Mouffetard. Good place for lunch or dinner.

VELLU

12 Rue de Mirbel, tel. 402-64-89. Small place, small price, great chef. See page 146.

CREPERIE DE LA MOUFFE

18 Rue Mouffetard, tel. 325-09-10. See page 157. A small, friendly, inexpensive crêperie.

AUTOGRAPHES
ETIENNE CHARAVAY
AU PREMIER A GAUCHE
ESCAL A DROI
dans la C

Glossary

The following is a list of words from this book that you may wish to use. We have tried to write the pronunciation in English, and, although it leaves much to be desired, those who have tried it were not incomprehensible. Remember to read the pronunciation instructions in English. No one syllable should be accented more than any other. The sound "zh" equals the sound of "s" in Parisian; the capital letter says its letter name. The "n" is lost somewhere in the nose. Add a throaty "r" and you are practically speaking French.

amitié (ah-meet-yay) friendship

ancien régime (ahn-C-N ray-zheem) the old regime, before 1789

apéritif (ah-pay-ree-teef) before-dinner drink

appartement (ah-par-te-mahn) apartment

à point (ah pwan) rare (meat)

beignet (ben-yeh) fritter

bidet (bee-day) oblong basin for washing private parts

bien cuit (byen kwee) well-cooked (meat)

bifteck (beef-take) steak

boeuf (berf) beef

boules (bool) the game of bowls

bouquiniste (boo-keen-eest) bookstall dealer

bric (breek) a Greek dish of lamb in pastry

café (kaff-A) coffee or a coffee house

café au lait (kaff-A O lay) coffee with milk

calembour (kahl-ahm-boor) rebus

carafe (kah-rahf) wine bottle

carnet (kar-neh) book of tickets

casse-croûte (kahss-kroot) long sandwich

caveau (kahv-O) cellar, often used to refer to night clubs *chambre* (shahm-bre) room or hotel room

chère (share) dear

charcuterie (shar-cute-er-E) delicatessen

clochard (klush-R) vagrant

collège (kull-ezh) secondary school

contrôle (kun-troll) supervisor

coq au vin (kuck O van) chicken in wine sauce

coquille (kuck-E) scallop shell

correspondence (koh-resp-own-dahnce) change point on the subway

cours (koor) courtyard or classes

crème chantilly (krem shahn-T-yee) whipped cream

crème fraiche (krem fresh) heavy cream

crèmerie (krem-er-E) dairy

crêpe (krep) French pancake

crêperie (krep-er-E) pancake restaurant

croissant (krwah-sahn) pastry roll

demi(e) (deu-mee) half

direction (D-wreck-tsee-own) the name of the terminal point of the subway line a station is on

Ecole des Beaux Arts (A-kull day Boze R) School of Fine Arts

en brochette (on brush-ette) cooked on a spit

enseigne (on-sen-yuh) sign, standard

entrecôte (on-tre-coat) rib steak

entresol (on-truh-sull) mezzanine

escalier à claire voie (S-kahl-yay ah clair vwah) open staircase

escalier à vis (S-kahl-yay ah vees) spiral staircase

espadrille (S-pah-dree) canvas shoe with a rope sole

esprit de corps (S-pree de core) team spirit

filet mignon (fee-leh mean-yone) fillet of beef

flambé (flahm-bay) flamed dish

flambiche (flahm-beesh) fruit pudding

flipper (flee-pair) pinball machine

genre (zhan-re) kind, species

gitane (zhee-tahn) gypsy; a brand of cigarette

habitué (ah-bit-U-A) regular customer

hôtel (O-tell) hotel

interdit (an-tair-D) forbidden

intime (an-team) intimate

jeton (zhuh-tone) token

maison (may-zone) house

maître d'hôtel (met-ruh doh-tell) major domo

mal au foie (mahl O fwah) liver trouble

marchand de vins (marsh-on de van) wine dealer

marché (marsh-A) market place

mascaron (mahsk-R-own) grotesque face or figure; a mask

mercerie (mare-sir-E) dry goods store

métro (may-trow) subway

mignon (mean-yone) delicate, pretty one

moufette (moof-ette) skunk

oubliette (oo-blee-ette) dungeon

parfumerie (pah-fume-er-E) perfumery

parvis (pahr-V) open space in front of a church

pâté (pah-tay) meat pie

petit (put-E) little

petit dejeuner (put-E day-zhuhn-A) breakfast

pneumatique (pnoo-mah-teek) message sent by tube

pommes frites (pum freet) French fried potatoes

pont (pohn) bridge

porte-cochères (port kush-air) carriage entrance

pounti (poon-T) name of a vegetable pie

pour parler appuyez (pour parl-A ahp-we-A) push in order to speak

pré aux clercs (pray O clare) meadow for students

premier étage (pree-me-air A-tahzh) first floor

prix fixe (pree feex) fixed price

quart (kahr) quarter

quartier (cart-yay) neighborhood

raison d'être (ray-zone det-ruh) reason for being

rez de chausée (red-show-say) ground floor

ris de veau (ree de voh) sweetbreads

sabot (sab-O) boot

saignant (sen-yahn) very rare (meat)

sarrasin (sah-rah-zan) buckwheat

service (sair-veese) service

service compris (sair-veese kum-pree) service included in the bill

signe (see-nyuh) sign

sommelier (sum-el-yay) wine steward

spécialité de la maison (spess-E-ahl-E-teh de la may-zone) specialty of the
   house

tabac (tah-bah) tobacco; tobacco shop

tarte aux blettes (tart O blette) a strawberry spinach pie

terminal (tair-mean-ahl) end of the subway line

CHRONOLOGY

52—the Roman invasion of Lutèce

Fourth century—the city received the name of Paris

481-511—Reign of Clovis

511-558—Reign of Childebert, the son of Clovis

886—Norman invasion

1180-1223—Reign of Phillip Augustus

1547-1559—Reign of Henry II and Catherine de Médicis

1574-1589—Reign of Henry III

1589-1610—Reign of Henry IV. He was married to Marguerite de
Valois (*chère* Margot) until 1599, then to Marie de Médicis.
Marguerite de Valois was the daughter of Henry II and Catherine de
Médicis; she was the sister of Henry III and the cousin and wife of
Henry of Navarre, later Henry IV.

1610-1643—Reign of Louis XIII

1643-1715—Reign of Louis XIV
Madame de Montespan was a favorite of Louis XIV by whom she had
eight children.
Madame de Maintenon was the tutor of Louis XIV's children by
Madame de Montespan. She secretly married him in 1697.

1715-1774—Reign of Louis XV

1774-1791—Reign of Louis XVI. He was guillotined by the
Revolutionary government at the Place de la Concorde.

1789-1799—French Revolution

1793-1794—Reign of Terror. In 420 days 2,669 people were condemned and executed.
Robespierre was a Revolutionary leader and member of the Committee
of Public Safety who was responsible for the Terror.

1795-1799—Directory

1799-1804—Consulate under Napoleon Bonaparte

1804-1814—Empire, with Napoleon as emperor

1852-1870—Reign of Napoleon III
Georges Haussman was city planner for Napoleon III from 1853-1870.

1968—Evènements de Mai, student riots in Paris

INDEX OF STREET NAMES, STORES, AND RESTAURANTS